Gain Save Give

DOING THE RIGHT THING
WITH MONEY

Peter Dixon

Cloudshill Press

LONDON CHELTENHAM

Copyright © 2020 by Peter Dixon.

All rights reserved. No part of this publication may be reproduced, distributed or transmitted in any form or by any means, including photocopying, recording, or other electronic or mechanical methods, without the prior written permission of the publisher, except in the case of brief quotations embodied in critical reviews and certain other noncommercial uses permitted by copyright law. For permission requests, please contact the publisher by email.

Scripture quotations marked (NIV) are taken from the Holy Bible, New International Version®, NIV®. Copyright © 1973, 1978, 1984, 2011 by Biblica, Inc.™ Used by permission of Zondervan. All rights reserved worldwide. www.zondervan.com The "NIV" and "New International Version" are trademarks registered in the United States Patent and Trademark Office by Biblica, Inc.™

Scripture quotations marked (MSG) are taken from *THE MESSAGE*, copyright © 1993, 2002, 2018 by Eugene H. Peterson. Used by permission of Navpress. All rights reserved. Represented by Tyndale House Publishers.

Peter Dixon/Cloudshill Press

27, Old Gloucester Street, LONDON, WC1N 3AX, UK

E: info@cloudshillpress.com   www.cloudshillpress.com

Book Layout ©2015 BookDesignTemplates.com

Ordering Information: For quantity sales, please contact the publisher by email at info@cloudshillpress.com.

Gain Save Give / Peter Dixon —1st ed.

ISBN   978-1-9160273-6-7 (paperback)
        978-1-9160273-8-1 (ebook)

Contents

Introduction 5
Gain 15
Save 39
Give 79
Bringing it all together 103
Acknowledgments 111
Resources 113
    Web resources 113
    Personal finance software 121
    Further reading 122
    Budget Categories 124
John Wesley's 'The Use of Money' 127

For Ingrid

Whatever your heart clings to and confides in, that is really your God.

– MARTIN LUTHER (1483-1546)

CHAPTER 1

Introduction

John Wesley and money

IN THE SPRING OF 1726, Samuel Wesley was proud of his son. John had just accepted the prestigious fellowship of Lincoln College, Oxford, to start in the autumn. The position would in due course attract a range of obscure allowances, for laundry, salt and other expenses. They would keep John's finances more or less afloat when the college eventually paid them, but there was just one problem. John was penniless.

Samuel, himself the worst of money managers, raised a loan to help out. But the only way John could survive the summer was to spend it at his parents' country parsonage on the other side of the country. John had no money to pay for a seat in a carriage. He made the 140-mile journey from Oxford to Epworth in Lincolnshire on foot.

Once he arrived at the family home, he worked hard to earn his keep in the efficient household run by his mother, Susanna. The twenty-fourth child of a nonconformist minister, Susanna Wesley was a strict parent and a spirited woman. She was also patient with her husband's almost permanent indebtedness, even when he spent three months in the Lincoln debtors' prison. Regarding money, their fourteenth child, John, learned lessons both from his father's terrible example and his mother's guidance.

Susanna Wesley (Public Domain)

We may not think of John Wesley when we are looking for a personal-finance role model. A key figure in the history of the Protestant church, Wesley was the founder of Methodism. He preached against the shallow nominal Christianity that abounded in eighteenth-century

England. Born in June 1703, he went to the English public school Charterhouse and then studied at Christ Church in Oxford, where he eventually took up the fellowship of Lincoln College. Along the way, he was ordained as an Anglican priest. While at Oxford, he was a member of the Holy Club, whose members covenanted with each other to pursue a Christian life as devoutly as they could.

Wesley travelled around Britain and Ireland on horseback, preaching outdoors in open spaces to all who would listen. He could not preach in churches; most local ministers would not open their pulpits to him. In October 1735, he and his younger brother Charles sailed to Savannah, Georgia, to serve the inhabitants. His stay there lasted from February 1736 to December of the following year, when a controversial dispute with the colonists forced his return to England.

Statue of John Wesley, Indiana (Public Domain)

Wesley gave thousands of sermons. In one of them, he described his personal rule about money:

Having,

First, gained all you can, and,

Secondly saved all you can,

Then give all you can.[1]

Wesley observed that secular philosophers and poets called wealth 'the pest of all society', a source of evil. On the other hand, Christian preachers and teachers did not give money the importance it deserved. Money was embarrassing. Best not talked about. For Wesley, it was the love of money that corrupted a person. The fault lay not with the money itself, but rather with those who misused it. He translated this belief into a set of rules for personal finance that he applied to his own life with consistency and perseverance. To update these principles to the twenty-first century is the aim of this book.

Modern context

I sometimes wonder how Wesley would see today's world, and our churches. He would not recognise the technology, of course, but he would have much to say about our attitude to money. The coronavirus pandemic has knocked us back. As I write, I have no idea how 'normal' life can ever be again. Many have lost relatives to

---

[1] Unless otherwise stated, quotations from John Wesley are from his sermon *The Use of Money*.

the virus. Some are still affected by 'long Covid', experiencing symptoms doctors find difficult to explain. Others have been unable to earn a living.

Looking back, though, most people in Western Europe, North America and Australia have enjoyed increasing prosperity for sixty years or longer. Yet the more we have, the more we seem to want. Yesterday's luxury is today's essential.

Many have been left behind. Improving economies should have reduced inequality, but it has increased. The same is even more true internationally. Where the benefits of globalisation have spread to the developing world at all, they have too often stayed with the privileged and not filtered down to the poorest. Whether it's food or housing, there's enough in the world to go around, if only we would share it around.

Don't imagine that I'm saying this from some moral high ground. I have more to learn than most from John Wesley about money. And I find it as difficult as anyone else.

It's difficult

What makes it so difficult to keep our finances under control? Why are so many of us up to our eyeballs in debt?

All of us find it difficult to control money, but some have it worse than others. Many struggle to make ends meet from one payday to the next. Families on a low income, from a low-paid job or from benefit, just don't have enough money coming in to feed the children. They face daily choices between eating or heating, shopping for essentials or paying the rent. Luxuries are not an option.

But that may not be our situation. We may have a steady income and a good job. Even so, we still find it hard to control our spending. There's always something else that we must have, something we absolutely need. Perhaps it's about keeping up appearances. If our neighbour has something, we have to have it too. Or a better version: the latest fashion, the newest car, the most capable mobile phone. Peer pressure is a very potent force. It's most powerful among teenagers, but it affects us at any age.

The environment we exist in today makes this even more difficult. It's so easy to buy something. Advertisers bombard us, on television, in magazines, in newspapers. Our credit cards allow us to put off the reckoning to the distant future. But there will be a reckoning. Before we know where we are, the debt has piled up and has become uncontrollable.

If debt is your particular problem, you'll find some ideas for getting it under control in the following chapters, and the Appendix has suggestions for where you can get help. Perhaps your income is very low and you struggle to stay afloat financially. If so, you may think some of the ideas in the book don't apply to you. But I hope you will be encouraged to find ways to make the best of the resources you have. Again, the links in the Appendix will prove helpful.

Jesus was talking about our ambivalent relationship with money in Mark's gospel (Mark: 4:19) when he spoke of the deceitfulness of wealth. Whenever we have money, it slips easily through our fingers.

Even the people who claim they can help us do a better job with our finances make good money out of us, whether we flourish or hit hard times.

What is this book for?

We've all seen those *Get Rich Quick* books. There are plenty of them on airport book stands (remember pre-Covid airports?), where travellers have time to browse. They have titles like '*Work for 4 hours a week and retire at 40!*' and '*You CAN be a Millionaire!*'. Perhaps nowadays it's 'billionaire'. There's inflation to deal with.

Ironically, one way to get rich is to sell books telling readers how to get rich (and then 'upsell' an expensive seminar or video training course). There's a personal finance industry, complete with its big names, its gurus, its jargon ('Minimalism', 'Financial Freedom', 'Financial Independence, Retire Early'), its shady characters, its snake oil salesmen.

This is not that kind of book. In *Gain Save Give*, I aim to help those who want to go a little further than 'just' getting rich. Because when you have all that money, what are you going to do with it? When you've retired at 45, what will you do with all that time? It's just as important to deal with your money and other resources wisely - yes, even generously - as to acquire everything you can.

The purpose of this book is to translate Wesley's good counsel - 'Having first gained all you can and secondly saved all you can, then give all you can' - into practical advice for those of us who want to make the best use of the resources with which we have been entrusted. For money, like every resource, is a gift that God expects us to steward - an important word - as effectively as we can.

In the following chapters we will discover how to put Wesley's advice into practice in a world in which many of us are tempted to look out for ourselves, to consume everything that advertisers offer us. I believe we can resist the pressures we face every day and become the generous men and women God calls us to be. What we shouldn't do is pretend that money is unimportant. It's one of the issues most often mentioned in the Bible.

John Wesley suggests that people in the church don't think enough about money. They don't think it is important enough to worry about. They don't think of how they should use it to the best long-term advantage. And they don't think of what 'long-term' means. (Hint: it doesn't end when we die.)

We read that the love of money is the root of all evil, but not that money itself is evil. As Wesley says, the fault does not lie in the money, but in them that use it. Like anything, money can be used badly. But it can just as easily be used well. Well, perhaps not quite as easily.

Money is the means by which we transact business of every kind. It's also a way and means of doing good, or as Wesley says 'all manner of good'. We can use money to feed the hungry, to provide drink for the thirsty, to provide clothing for those who have none. It can provide travellers with somewhere to lay their heads. As Wesley says, by it we may supply the place of husband to the widow or father to the fatherless. Those are powerful and positive possibilities.

So we need to know how to employ this invaluable resource. And Wesley suggests that all the instruction needed to make best use of this resource comprises three things: gain all you can; save all you can; and give all you can.

That is what I want to look into in this book. Wesley's primary focus in the sermon was money, but he talked about other resources too. I too will consider how we can be better stewards of resources like time and the space in our homes and gardens, as well as the money with which they are linked.

I focus this book on the key points of John Wesley's sermon. Each of the next three chapters deals with one of Wesley's areas and concludes with some ideas for concrete action. I include some quite self-evident ideas, more as reminders than to claim any originality. Some useful resources to support these actions are in the Appendix.

The principles of John Wesley's sermon and, I hope, the contents of this book are firmly rooted in the Christian scripture. But you will find few references to specific biblical verses. Where those of other religions, or none, have something from which we can learn, I take advantage of it.

Wesley addressed his sermon to Christians, and much of the advice that he gives has that focus. But I hope that his wise counsel, brought up to date, applies to anybody who wishes to do good with their money, whether it's a lot or not very much: not only to look after their family, which is crucial, but also to make best use of the resources they have at their disposal, even if they do not see those resources as a gift from God. Whether you are Christian, Muslim, Jewish, Hindu or a humanist, I hope you will gain something from this attempt to look at how best to use money: how to gain, how to save and not to waste, so we can give.

CHAPTER 2

Gain

'GAIN ALL YOU CAN', EXHORTED JOHN WESLEY. He said it was every Christian's duty to do so.

It doesn't sound very Christian, somehow. It seems too greedy. Aren't we supposed to deny ourselves? Didn't Jesus tell us: 'Watch out! Be on your guard against all kinds of greed; life does not consist in an abundance of possessions' (Luke 12:15, NIV). Well, Wesley went on to say how to make those gains ('by honest industry') and what we should do with them. The advice on what to do with wealth, be it ever so small, comes later. In this chapter, though, we need to look at what Wesley meant by 'gain all you can'.

Almost in the same breath, he talked about diligence and avoiding diversions, procrastination and half-measures. He talked about common sense, education and making the best of our resources and talents.

Gaining industriously

> *'Genius is nothing but labour and diligence'.*
> *William Hogarth (1697-1764).*

Wesley himself was nothing if not diligent. He 'combined a genius for organization with an irresistible dynamism'. He was 'a man of action who would ride a hundred miles in a day, stopping only to change horses and preach along the way'.[2] Today, our 'riding' may depend on transport with rather more horsepower. We have it easy by comparison, but the principles of work have changed little.

I'm reminded of a stonemason's comment, no doubt made by many an artisan in stone from the twelfth century to the present day. Canadian John Gilbert describes visiting Tewkesbury Abbey in the west of England with his stonemason uncle. They climbed up into the gallery high above the nave. John admired the beautiful carvings. 'But no one can see them', he said. 'Ah, but God can', replied his uncle.[3]

Diligence is taking the trouble, attending to the detail, making the effort, doing excellent work even if no human will see it for the next 500 years. 'Do nothing by halves', said Wesley. It may not be the way we run our businesses, schools or governments in our high-speed world, but I don't want to get nostalgic for slower times. In any case,

---

[2] Roy Hattersley (2002), *A Brand from the Burning: the life of John Wesley*, London, Little & Brown, pp. 3-4.

[3] John H V Gilbert, Letter to the *Financial Times*, 27th April 2019.

some of us are detail people, some more interested in the big picture. I'm in the second group, so I sometimes have to tell myself to slow down and deal with the details. Many's the time I've uploaded a document and then noticed a minor error. Even worse is to send an email attachment with errors in it. Or no attachment at all; we've all done that. So exercising diligence can pay off even in the short term. You may not be around in a century or two to be told that you made a mistake in your stone carving, but it would be good if the boss didn't call to point out your silly errors.

On the other hand, the finer points of a problem can be a distraction from the big picture. That's the other extreme. Especially if you are one of those detail people, it's all too easy to spend your time enjoying the minutiae of your work. Are you avoiding dealing with the big stuff?

I'm not talking about distractions, which Wesley also warns against. It is of course important to focus. Delving into new knowledge, for instance, can be fun even if it's a wild goose chase. The internet is our enemy here. You can spend hours doing 'research' without ever achieving a single useful result. I know! I've been there.

As Wesley puts it, we should 'lose no time in silly diversions'. Hard to believe he had not heard of Facebook, Whatsapp, Snapchat or Instagram. Still, increasing addiction to social media - teenagers spending nine hours a day on social media and becoming anxious if they can't get access for an hour - is not our subject here.

Distractions aside, even well-focused attention to detail can have its downside. 'He can't see the wood for the trees' is such a cliché that I hesitate to use it, but it hits the spot - to use another one.

Wesley helps us out again. Twice, actually. First, he advises us to 'Use all the common sense that God has given you'. Clearly, it is not really diligence to count every blade of grass on the football field and never reach the goal (or a touchdown, depending on what kind of football you have in mind). That's a crazy exaggeration, of course, a kind of *reductio ad absurdum* to make the point, but we are in good company. Jesus did it constantly.

This is where another piece of John Wesley's advice comes into play. Money is not the only resource entrusted to us as stewards. There's time, too. Minutes add up to hours, hours to days. If we spend all our time on the tiny details, we will either run out of time to get the job done, or run ourselves ragged with overwork and stress. We reach the destination exhausted. 'Lose no time', said Wesley, but he also told his hearers to use their common sense.

We have to get the balance right between detail and big picture, between the small stuff and the big stuff, between tactics and strategy. We have to follow a 'third way', neither ignoring the detail (as I sometimes do) nor losing sight of the '30,000-foot view'. Whatever the subject, most of us tend to one extreme or the other if we don't think things through. Perhaps most of us tend towards getting lost in the detail. There's so much information out there. Some of it is even true.

'Make the best of all that is in your hands', was John Wesley's counsel. Unfortunately, what was in his hands then - at least in terms of information - was a tiny fraction of that put before us each day. So first we have to discern what is 'fake news', and whether the person who claims that the news is fake has a record of truth-telling. Ultimately, though, it is for us to use our judgement and 'common sense', a much harder task than in the eighteenth century. However we discern this, we will end up with a collection of resources: a mass of data; our own talents and capabilities, money and other physical resources; and of course time.

One useful tool is the famous 'Pareto Principle', otherwise known as the '80/20 Rule'. Economist Vilfredo Pareto originally devised it to describe inequitable land ownership in Italy, but we use it today to suggest that 80% of outputs derive from 20% of the inputs. The application to time management and how we apply our effort is obvious. If we choose the right focus, 20% of our work could drive 80% of the successful outcomes. By focusing on the most important tasks during our working hours, we can hit that 20/80 sweet spot. We 'just' have to step back and get the right 20%. That's the hard part, but it's worth it.

Reformer John Wesley gave much more advice relevant here, but we will return to it later. There will be a section looking at 'lifelong learning', which may not seem to have much to do with 'Gain, Save, Give'. The relevance will become clear.

'Study continually that you may improve on those who have gone before you', was how Wesley put it.

He also said something that we could easily miss on a

cursory reading: 'Use all possible diligence *in your calling*'. I look briefly at the idea of 'calling' or vocation in the next section, and near the end of the book we visit the 'stages of life' everyone passes through; 'do not put off until tomorrow what may be done today', was Wesley's take on this.

Gaining through work

'Contentment makes poor men rich, discontent makes rich men poor.' Benjamin Franklin (1706-1790).

How you gain money - and the power that it may bring - is crucial. Is it through hard work, or just an accident of birth? John Locke said, 'All wealth is the product of labour', but that begs a question: 'Your own labour or someone else's?'. Family money, 'old money': we might envy someone their inheritance, but not always with justification.

William Shakespeare deals with the theme of inheritance in several of his plays: the murderous Macbeth has no offspring to whom to bequeath his throne; Portia in *The Merchant of Venice* inherits wealth, but also a marriage trap devised by her now dead father; the plots of the history plays *Richard II* and *Richard III* turn on the corruption and greed spawned by potential inheritance.

The Bard's modern namesake Nicholas Shakespeare tells a different story in his book *Inheritance*. The central character, underpaid Andy Larkham, one day makes a simple mistake that makes him £17 million richer. Andy wants to attend the funeral of his former teacher, but sits down in the wrong chapel. Just one other mourner is present. Andy signs the register and leaves. He thinks little more of his error, until he learns that the deceased, a lonely millionaire, has left his fortune to anyone who attends his funeral. There's much more to the story than that, but it deals with the dangers of unexpected and unearned wealth. Perhaps you dream of winning the lottery or inheriting a massive amount of money. Be careful what you wish for! Inherited wealth can be as much of a curse as a blessing.

You may or may not see yourself as wealthy. If you do, you may have gained your wealth by inheritance, by canny investment, through the house price inflation enjoyed by the baby-boomer generation, or by the 'sweat of your brow'. Those differences will shape your thinking about money.

Let's not forget that most of us in the developed world are rich by global standards. If you own your home, even with a mortgage, you are in the top 1-2% in the world. But even by the standards of your own society, you may be 'comfortably off'. What you do with that wealth is a theme of a later chapter. For now, I want to think about our responsibility to our sons and daughters, if we are fortunate enough to have them.

You may not be doing your children a favour by passing on a great deal of wealth to them, whether during your lifetime or at its end. Younger readers may not want to hear this, but it's true. Parents do of course have a responsibility to provide for their families, but history and literature are full of examples of young men and women who have veered off the rails because their financial life was too easy.

The young man we know as the Prodigal Son (Luke 15:11-32) was one. Jesus tells his story primarily to show God's willingness to forgive. But the parable also emphasises the need to turn away from foolish extravagance. The wandering wastrel has to reach rock bottom before he can learn this lesson. Those who gain wealth without having to work for it need to watch out.

How do you view your work? You may not enjoy commuting to the office every day (or sitting in front of a screen all day, as is more likely the case in Covidland). Many jobs are boring and repetitive. The *FIRE* movement, *Financial Independence Retire Early*, rests on our desire to escape from worthless or mind-numbing work.

I'm not convinced that retiring to a life of leisure is the nirvana that the early retiree expects. More successful is a transition to activity that is a closer match for someone's gifts, skills and aptitudes, something right for their stage of life. I sometimes think that I'm currently in my third career; I'm not sure I'll ever truly retire.

Work - the right work - is a good thing. From the second chapter of Genesis onward, the Bible tells us this. But how do we find work and what kind of work do we find? While I'm not a fan of introspection - 'navel-gazing' - there is a place for examining 'who we are and what we are called to be and do'.

Some years ago, my wife and I had the privilege of attending a Summer School retreat at Schloss Mittersill in Austria. One speaker, Gordon Smith, gave a thoughtful and inspiring series of talks on vocation, which helped me to clarify my thinking about work, leisure and family.

I returned to Smith's ideas subsequently, when I found that he had distilled the talks into a book. I sought out a second-hand copy. The concepts are biblical and Smith's examples come from church, missionary and academic experience, but the principles are valid whatever the reader's belief system. Smith's book, *Courage and Calling*, appeared in 1999 but is packed with a wisdom that remains fresh today. It repays reflective reading.

You might think that this kind of reflection is relevant only to those who are starting out on a career. I disagree. It is never too late to rethink our direction. We can hope that advancing years will bring maturity. But they may also free us from responsibility for a young family and open up new opportunities. Whether we use that for leisure or a different but productive path is a choice.

There may not be much choice right now. Our options depend on our health, talents and the resources at our disposal in this moment. But we will see in later chapters that those too may be under our control. Perhaps we need to be patient, and start a process that will pay off later.

Gaining constructively

'The worship of the golden calf of old has found a new and heartless image in the cult of money and the dictatorship of an economy which is faceless and lacking any truly human goal.' Pope Francis (b. 1936).

How we make our living matters. Some jobs and professions are exploitative and destructive. Some are damaging to us. You might disagree about what they are.

But if we've thought about it at all, we all draw the line somewhere.

John Wesley did. In his sermon on money, Wesley suggests that 'We ought to gain all we can gain, without buying gold too dear, without paying more for it than it is worth'. Even the potential for gaining enormous sums of money, he says, should not tempt us to take on an employment that damages our health, our minds or our neighbour.

Gaining safely

'I believe that the greatest gift you can give your family and the world is a healthy you.' Joyce Meyer (b. 1943).

John Wesley was a practical man. Health came first. Our personal circumstances shape our thinking, and this was true for him. All that walking and - when he could eventually afford a horse - all those miles on horseback meant he needed to conserve his fitness if he was to do his work for God. Even in his early years at Oxford, he was preoccupied with health, as well as with his lack of money.

Although something of a hypochondriac, the young John had good cause to worry about his health: biliousness, frequent nosebleeds. Later he took advice from the writings of a 'Dr Cheyne' - plenty of exercise, temperance, the right food - advice we could usefully follow today.

What has this to do with our work? Wesley's point was that we should not continue in, or even start, an occupation that is damaging to our bodies.

This might mean the potential for direct injury, such as working with hazardous machinery or material. As the first shoots of the Industrial Revolution peeped through in eighteenth-century Britain, this would become more and more of an issue during Wesley's lifetime. Many of the workers labouring in dangerous mines, factories and mills had little choice. This might be the only way they could earn even a subsistence wage and support their families.

There are more options today. Safety and working conditions have improved dramatically. Tiny children no longer have to work in our factories or climb up chimneys to clean out the soot. (But children still work in sweatshops in many countries, and we might be taking advantage of cheap prices and wearing the clothes they have made.) Speaking from a position of relative privilege in a country that is more prosperous than most, I have to be careful what I say. Yet even if you are less fortunate, you may have choices. Only you can know how much freedom you have to stay away from work that may directly damage your health. As John Wesley put it:

> Some employments are absolutely and totally unhealthy; as those which imply the dealing much with arsenic, or other equally hurtful minerals, or the breathing an air tainted with steams of melting lead, which must at length destroy the firmest constitution.

Then there is the more indirect damage. Our work can damage our health in much less obvious ways, as Wesley points out. 'No gain whatsoever', he said,

> should induce us to enter into, or to continue in, any employ, which is of such a kind, or is attended with so hard or so long labour, as to impair our constitution. Neither should we begin or continue in any business which necessarily deprives us of proper seasons for food and sleep, in such a proportion as our nature requires.

So Wesley recognised the importance of getting enough rest. A job that requires us to work long hours, or to keep going every day without rest, is damaging in the long term. Whether we are fans of 'keeping Sunday special' or not, the idea of taking at least one day's rest each week is not in the Bible by accident. It makes sense for human wellbeing.

Wesley did not, of course, know about our more modern dangers: our sitting for hours without a break in front of a computer screen; our employers' expectation that we are constantly reachable by smartphone; our permanent obsession with checking emails; our stress-related snacking on food laden with hidden sugar. But he would have had something to say about those hazards too.

Actually, he sort of did. He talked about occupations that 'require many hours to be spent in writing; especially if a person write sitting, and lean upon his stomach, or remain long in an uneasy posture'.

> Whatever it is which reason or experience shows to be destructive of health or strength, that we may not submit to; seeing "the life is more valuable than meat, and the body than raiment". And if we are already engaged in such an employ, we should exchange it as soon as possible for some which, if it lessen our gain, will however not lessen our health.

Wesley was uncompromising. 'If our reason or experience shows that a job is unhealthy for us', he said, 'then we should leave it as soon as possible even if this means that our income is reduced'. Our own circumstances may not allow us to change jobs, at least at the moment.

As I write, the coronavirus pandemic has put many livelihoods in jeopardy. Even if things return to 'normal', financial commitments may prevent such a drastic remedy. But we can at least recognise the problem and start a process of change.

Gaining honestly

'When wealth is lost, nothing is lost; when health is lost, something is lost; when character is lost, all is lost.' Billy Graham (1918-2018).

You could come up with many arguments for not taking up dishonest employment. The one you might not have thought of is the damage to ourselves. John Wesley does not start from the premise that breaking the law is simply wrong. He suggests we should not pursue any trade 'that is contrary to the law of God, or of our country' because it might prevent us from preserving 'the spirit of an healthful mind'. We can perhaps see where he is coming from.

Of course, Wesley does see these things as wrong in themselves. But whether or not we are found out, prosecuted and sent to prison, gaining a dishonest living will in the long run affect our minds and our character. As Wesley puts it, 'to gain money we must not lose our souls'.

You might not be thinking of taking up the 'trade' of burglary, fencing stolen goods or bank robbery. Yet it is worth examining how much we are tempted to take the easier, less honest option.

The working environment can make those choices extremely difficult. Issues like the tax system can make dishonesty the norm. I recall a conversation with a Christian entrepreneur trying to lead a small business in Hungary, as the country emerged from decades of Communism. Tax rates were ridiculously high, but businesspeople grasped opportunities to evade tax through endless loopholes, through falsifying tax returns and expense receipts, or even through bribery. 'It's almost impossible to run an honest business here', he complained, 'to make even a tiny profit you have to cheat'.

You don't have to be an entrepreneur to face these challenges. They may arise in day-to-day life as employees in a large organisation. Perhaps you will encounter 'minor' adjustments of expense claims. The culture of the organisation is crucial. 'Everybody does it'; if you don't go along, you're letting the team down. John Wesley has an answer. Avoid 'conformity to some custom', he says, 'which is not consistent with a good conscience'. Clear enough.

And then there are taxes. Whether employees or independent traders, most of us pay them. You can legitimately arrange your affairs to pay as little tax as possible. That's fine, and perfectly legal. There is a line, though, that we should not cross. 'It is at least as sinful', says the eighteenth-century John Wesley, 'to defraud the king of his right, as to rob our fellow subjects'. The government - Wesley's 'king' - has 'full as much right to his customs [taxes] as we have to our houses and apparel'. Quite clear, although we will come upon questions that straddle the border of legality. Conscience will guide us.

We will need to consider our situation carefully. Some businesses or employments may be 'innocent in themselves', but 'cannot be followed with innocence'. And there may be occupations in which you become involved with an 'in crowd' - to use an old-fashioned phrase - that sucks you into a way of life that threatens your character. Avoid it, says Wesley.

In some ways, though, Wesley draws a more subtle line. Presumably taking a lead from Chapter 8 of the first letter to the Corinthians, where the issue is what kind of food we may eat, he suggests that a fixed rule may not work for everyone. Some occupations may be fine for one person but hazardous to another. It may be about the company you will have to keep or something about your own character that raises the red flag, 'a peculiarity in your constitution of soul', as Wesley puts it, 'by reason whereof that employment is deadly to you, which another may safely follow'. You might come up with examples - an alcoholic in a distillery, a gambling addict in a casino, a chocoholic in Charlie's factory - but ultimately each person probably knows or quickly learns what career decision may be a deadly mistake.

Wesley had his own example. He was 'convinced, from many experiments', that he 'could not study, to any degree of perfection, either mathematics, arithmetic, or algebra'. Yet others 'may study them all their lives without sustaining any inconvenience'. Who knows what he found hazardous about mathematics? Mathematicians reading this book can probably rest easy and not rush off to find another occupation.

As Wesley says, 'None therefore can here determine for another; but every man must judge for himself, and abstain from whatever he in particular finds to be hurtful to his soul'.

Gaining fairly

> *'A sterling reputation is better than striking it rich; a gracious spirit is better than money in the bank.'* Proverbs 22:1 (MSG).

> *'What is true of ourselves is equally true of our neighbour. We should not "gain all we can" by causing injury to another, whether to his trade, his body or his soul.'*

> John Wesley, The Use of Money

There are many ways in which our work can harm others. Some of us may be in a profession that includes the possibility of harming others physically, such as the military or the police. Plenty of material exists on when that may be justified, a controversial issue that is outside our scope here.[4] For most of us, though, our harm to others is more indirect.

Through our 'trade' we may cause others harm without even realising it. According to John Wesley, we

---

[4] I have written on this in *Peacemakers: A Christian View of War and Peace*, Cheltenham, Cloudshill Press, Peter Dixon (2019).

'should not sell our goods below their market price'. That's difficult to understand in terms of modern global markets. Take it as covering all kinds of 'sharp practice'. What does it mean today? We can see this at two different levels: our own personal dealings and our national place in the global market.

We may not personally be in the business of selling goods to the public, although most of us have probably sold something on Ebay, Gumtree or perhaps just in a garage sale or yard sale. Selling too cheaply is unlikely to be a problem. The question for us is then more likely to be how accurately we describe what we sell and how trustworthy we are as sellers.

Wesley picks out a few examples of shady practice to beware of. All of them lead us back sooner or later to integrity.

Some are straightforward and translate directly to us if we do sell things, whether it is in a local store or a multi-million conglomerate business. 'It is quite wrong', he said, 'to make a living from selling those things which would harm a neighbour's health'. He would not have heard of 'use by' dates. A sniff test had to suffice for perishable foods. Other foods could contain hidden hazards. Today we don't have to worry about bread adulterated to look whiter, with chalk or an aluminium compound we now use in detergent. We need not concern ourselves about steep and narrow staircases that might cause fatal accidents, or the danger of fire caused by lighting our homes with candles. Warning labels and safer design protect us from hazards our forebears faced each day.

Perhaps the 'nannying' sometimes goes too far: 'Caution, the contents of this coffee cup may be hot'.

Even in modern life, though, we do face hazards. Let's not contribute to dangers to the health of others. I hope that another of hypochondriac Wesley's health concerns is less of an issue today. 'A physician', he said, 'should not deliberately prolong a patient's illness in order to improve his own income'. Take heed, if you are a doctor reading this! Actually, I've never yet met a physician who was anything but thoughtful and caring, but I suspect that was far from the case in the eighteenth century.

Today as then, though, all of us are in business, one way or another. We can heed John Wesley as he talks about trading practices. One clear example: we must not 'devour' someone else's land or house through gambling, through pawnbroking or through charging excessive interest on a loan. None of us does that, do we? Perhaps not personally, but give some thought to the policies of the company you work for and where your savings and retirement fund are invested. 'Ethical investment' can have all kinds of meanings. If we are in business for ourselves, what lengths do we go to, in order to turn a profit? Are we guilty of 'studying to ruin our neighbour's trade, in order to advance our own', as Wesley puts it. Or of 'enticing away or receiving any of his servants or workmen whom he has need of'. Maybe recruitment agencies and headhunters need to rethink how they ply their trade.

Not harming another's health or livelihood seems a straightforward concept, but Wesley also exhorts his listeners not to cause injury to others' souls. Here the ground is less firm. Yet there are examples. Some are obvious. You may not be a drug dealer or a loan shark. But are you in a business that encourages 'punters' to feed their addictions? Casinos spring to mind. Less extreme cases may not. Tobacco, alcohol, lotteries: all bear thinking about. Even more ambiguous are occupations that feed people's addiction to entertainment and pleasure. Nothing wrong with entertainment, of course, but the question may help us think about how much value our work brings to people's lives. I leave it to you to consider your individual situation. The clues are there.

These thoughts apply mostly to us as individuals, but that's a narrow field of view. If you are reading this in North America, Britain, Western Europe or Australia, you are among the richest people on the planet. Many argue that our wealth comes at the expense of the billions who live in poverty in the rest of the world. The number of billionaires is increasing, but this is not just about them. That would let us off the hook.

We can all do more to find out how we enjoy our way of life at the expense of those who struggle to find any employment at all from day to day, not to speak of good jobs. I will consider later what our giving can do towards redressing the balance. For now, we need to ask ourselves whether our work, whatever it may be, decreases or increases the gap between rich and poor. Strangely enough, this can even be in our own interests. Tackling global poverty at its roots, and the anger it engenders, can pay off. It may reduce some threats and concerns that make us so anxious today: migration, civil wars, terrorism.

We may feel helpless as individuals in the face of global forces. The difference we make may be small, but that does not make it worthless.

Our occupation is not so bad, though, is it? Perhaps we need to think more self-critically. The prophet Jeremiah suggested to one king of Judah that having 'more and more' did not make him a king, when his eyes and his heart were 'set only on dishonest gain, on shedding innocent blood and on oppression and extortion'. He compared the king with his father, who was satisfied with having enough to eat and drink, and who 'did what was right and just, so all went well with him'. He 'defended the cause of the poor and needy, and so all went well. 'Is that not what it means to know me?', declares the Lord'.

In the end, all of us could do worse than to subject every action, every aspect of our work, to Wesley's simple test. We will find it impossible to hurt others, directly or indirectly, he suggests, 'if we love our neighbour as ourselves'. Simple enough, but not so easy in practice.

Gaining enough

'To be clever enough to get all that money, one must be stupid enough to want it.' G.K. Chesterton (1874-1936).

How much is enough? It may be the wrong question to ask when you think about earning. It's true that the salaries people receive as CEOs of major corporations often seem obscenely high, compared with the men and women who work for them. Who can be worth $66 million a year? Or a 'severance package' of $10 million when being fired for under-performing? Yet the more important question is the one I will come on to in future chapters: what we do with the money.

For most of us, the problem of dealing with our millions doesn't arise. Indeed, we may be on low pay, finding it difficult getting to the end of each week. Luxuries are out of the question. The rest of us are probably somewhere in mid-range. We have enough to live on. But isn't there something else we 'need'?

The Australian comedian Barry Humphries, better known 'in character' as Dame Edna Everage, entitled his autobiography with admirable candour, *More Please*. I have always wanted more' he wrote.

> 'I never had enough milk or money or socks or sex or holidays or first editions or solitude or gramophone records or free meals or real friends or guiltless pleasure or neckties or applause or unquestioning love or persimmons. Of course, I have always had more than my share of most of these commodities but it always left me with a vague feeling of unfulfilment: where was the rest?'[5]

It's a cliché: 'Money isn't everything'.

Indeed, we can have too much of it. Those of us who are wealthy - that's you and I in our prosperous countries - are in danger: the danger of putting our trust in our possessions. In his powerful letter to a Jewish audience,

---

[5] More Please: An Autobiography, Barry Humphries (1993)

James shows how wealth makes it harder to avoid being greedy, arrogant and blind to the needs of others.[6]

In 1957, *Fortune* magazine named Jean Paul Getty the richest American then alive. The 1966 *Guinness Book of Records* claimed he was worth $1.2 billion, close to $10 billion in today's money. The Ridley Scott film *All the Money in the World* (2017) told how Getty refused to pay the demanded ransom for his kidnapped grandson. We may learn from Getty's frugality, but not from his personal life. In many ways, he saw himself as a failure. He married three times, and is famously quoted as saying, 'I would gladly give all of my millions for just one lasting marital success.'

So money really isn't everything. However little money we may have, we can be rich in our family and friends, our relationships, our health and our time. Success in our job or our business may come if we work with diligence, wisdom and fairness. But even if it does not, as Mother Teresa of Calcutta famously said, 'I am not called to be successful. I am called to be faithful.'

As the end of this chapter comes near, we have seen the different ways in which we can gain money and all those other resources. The Christian view on where the resources come from is clear. Everything we receive, whether we have sweated, given our time, or received an inheritance, comes as a gift of God. So as we look in the next chapter at saving, at looking after what we receive, we do so as stewards.

---

[6] James 5:.1–6.

Dietrich Bonhoeffer, in his book *The Cost of Discipleship*, comments on the sixth chapter of Matthew's gospel saying:

> Be not anxious! Earthly possessions dazzle our eyes and delude us into thinking that they can provide security and freedom from anxiety. Yet all the time they are the very source of all anxiety. If our hearts are set on them, our reward is an anxiety whose burden is intolerable. Anxiety creates its own treasures and they in turn beget further care. When we seek for security in possessions, we are trying to drive out care with care, and the net result is the precise opposite of our anticipations. The fetters which bind us to our possessions proved to be cares themselves.[7]

Or, as Plato put it more succinctly, 'The greatest wealth is to live content with little'.

Ideas for Action

- Is there anything about your working life that is damaging to your health? Monitor working time, eating habits, computer time, smartphone use. Make changes now.
- Research, reflect, and pray over how your job or trade contributes to other people's lives in your own country and elsewhere in the world, positively or negatively. Does your company deal honestly with the public, with suppliers, with competitors, with regulators? Discuss with your spouse and family

---

[7] Dietrich Bonhoeffer (1959), *The Cost of Discipleship*, New York, Macmillan, p. 158.

whether that should change.

- If you need a change, make a plan to achieve it in two years, five years, ten years. Even if you do not need to change direction, think about how you could work more diligently and strategically, applying the effort to 'the right 20%'.
- Give some thought to whether you are 'spoiling' your children by making their financial experiences too easy.
- Consider how you define success. Does money really make your world go round? Should it?
- Step back and reflect on 'who you are and what you are called to be'. Can you see yourself in the same occupation in ten years' time? If not, what would you need to do now to follow your calling? How do you 'get from here to there'? Are there actions you can take, financial savings you can make, educational paths you can start on (in your 'spare' time) now to reach a new goal?

CHAPTER 3

Save

'Do not throw [money] away in idle expenses, which is just the same as throwing it into the sea.' John Wesley.

THERE'S NO POINT IN GAINING ALL THAT MONEY if we just let it slip out of our fingers. Yet that's what many of us do. Even if we have a comfortable income, we don't seem to be able to hang on to it. Where does the money go? We need practical solutions to the problem of how to keep hold of our money once we've got it. In this chapter, I share some ideas on how to do that.

Saving consistently

'Annual income 20 pounds, annual expenditure 19 [pounds] 19 [shillings] and six [pence], result happiness. Annual income 20 pounds, annual expenditure 20 pounds ought and six, result misery.' Wilkins Micawber, fictional character in Charles Dickens' novel David Copperfield.

Mr Micawber has a simple approach to money: spending even a few pence or cents more than is coming in will eventually catch up with you.

It's obvious. We should not spend more than our income. But in a time of effortless credit, it's all too easy to do just that. So the first step in getting our finances under control is to know how much is coming in and how much is going out. If we don't budget, we can't save. If we don't save, we can't give.

Mr Wilkins Micawber, by Frank Reynolds (1876-1853), Public Domain

Budgeting is to some of us a scary word. It doesn't have to be so. There are many ways of managing a budget. You can just take a certain amount of cash out of the bank each week or month and only spend what's there. When it's gone, it's gone. But that's living in the past. Cash is becoming less and less part of our lives. Most of us live by our cards, or the even more modern Apple Pay and

Google Pay. Especially as coronavirus has brought many of us social distancing, contactless payment has rapidly become more crucial.

Some financial gurus will tell you: 'Ditch all your cards!' Perhaps you will have to, if uncontrolled spending is a habit you just can't beat. Yet debit cards and even credit cards can have their advantages. For most of us, they are an unavoidable part of modern life.

If you want to use credit cards to reap the benefits (airline miles, hotel points, cashback) and you're sure you can remain their master, fine. Just make sure you pay the bill in full every month. Otherwise, stick with debit cards.

Perhaps we can find a middle path, another 'third way'. We need to control the cards, not them us. The key is budgeting, but before we go there, let's look at the 'first fruits' idea.

Do you start the month with good intentions to save up for something and then realise as the days pass that there isn't a hope of achieving your goal? One solution is the biblical principle of 'first fruits'. More on this in the chapter on giving, but it applies just as well to saving.

The first fruits concept has a long history. Essentially, it means giving the first (and probably the best) portion of the harvest to God. The duty of tithing is based on it. Like it or not, peasants in the Middle Ages loaded part of their produce at harvest time into the local monastery's tithe barn to feed the monks.

Governments around the world use exactly this principle of first fruits to make sure they get their taxes. In Britain we call it Pay As You Earn; in the USA it's Tax

Withholding, in Canada it's Payroll Deduction. It's the same thing. The government will always make sure it gets its cut from the top of the pile. Before you even see the money, the tax man has got his pound of flesh.

Tithe barn, Lacock, England (author's photograph)

You can use the same system to build up your savings before you even see the money in the bank account. You can fool yourself. Just set up a regular payment into a savings account soon after payday and you won't even miss the money. Ten percent, twenty percent: it doesn't really matter how much, because you're probably going to change the amount fairly soon, as your budget settles down. Meanwhile, you'll be surprised how quickly you build up a nest egg fund.

So the automatic regular savings deduction is the first step in taking control. But you still need to know where all that money is disappearing to. You need a budget.

The next step is to go on a fact-finding mission. For at least a month, and preferably two or three, make an accurate record of all of your income and spending. Leave nothing out. Don't forget those cups of coffee on the way to work, the snacks during your work breaks, those coins put into a parking meter. If you're a family rather than an individual, you'll have to work together. Try to capture absolutely everything.

There are tools to help you do this. If you prefer old-fashioned paper, keep a small notebook with you. That's probably a good idea anyway, because you won't have a laptop with you every minute. At some point, though, you'll want to consolidate the results in a coherent way, to establish how much you are spending and on what.

The categories you choose will depend on your circumstances, but will include travel, utilities like water, heating and electricity, mortgage or rent, groceries, eating out, entertainment such as cinema and sports event tickets. You can find a detailed sample list in the Appendix.

Putting all of this together is where good personal finance software comes into its own. There are several options, some of which I mention in the Appendix. Many of them have ongoing costs. Personally, I use Acemoney, which does everything you might want and has a one-off price of around $45/£35. The free 'Lite' version has all the same functions, but you can only set up two accounts, such as 'Cash' and 'Bank'. That's not a bad way to start the process and decide whether the software meets your needs. Take a little time to work out which tools suit you best.

Armed with the right tools, it's time to act like Mr

Micawber. You're now ready to get an accurate picture of what you are spending and compare it with your income. If you are spending less than is coming in, congratulations! You have some headroom. If not, you're in an excellent position to find out where to tighten your belt. Do you need to buy lunch every day? Does anybody actually read those magazines and newspapers? Is that cable TV subscription still such great value since the six-month half-price deal ran out three years ago?

Spend some time balancing your budget, so that your income exceeds your spending, after allowing for at least modest 'first fruits' deductions into 'rainy day' savings - and giving. I will look further at giving in the next chapter, but this budget review is a good time to set up some giving 'off the top' as well as some saving.

If you follow this advice, you'll be setting yourself up to take control of your finances in the long term. After the first month or two, you won't need to go into as much detail. You can just record the major items, broadly estimate the rest and monitor how you get on. That time setting up your budget will have been a few hours well spent, helping you develop a habit that will pay off.

But even if your perusal of income and spending puts you on the 'result: happiness' side of the balance, you still need to work out where savings can be made. Looking at your record of spending will have given you a good idea of where the biggest categories of outgoings are. You're going to need that knowledge to save where it matters. Because saving is what we're about here. And how to do it better is the subject of the next section.

Saving by [not] spending

'Too many people spend money they haven't earned, to buy things they don't want, to impress people they don't like.'
Will Rogers (1879-1925).

Itinerant preacher John Wesley's characteristic appearance - untrimmed hair, lacking the then fashionable wig - had less to do with fashion and more to do with money. His mother, Susanna, thought that 'a visit to the barber would improve his energy'. He would have none of it. The 'more genteel appearance', he thought, was not 'sufficient grounds for spending two or three pounds more each year.

John Wesley preaching, Epworth, 1742 (Public Domain, Library of Congress).

'It was easy for him', we think. We face modern questions that John Wesley could not have even imagined. How many cars does your family need? Must you buy your cars new, when they lose almost a third of their value in the first year? Is there a public transport alternative? How about cycling? All of this depends on where we live and work. But those too are choices within our control, even if we can't change them overnight.

Then there's the mobile phone. It may be hard to survive today without a smartphone unless you withdraw from the world. But do you need the latest model, from the most fashionable company? Apple have skilfully created enticing brand appeal that draws you in like a magnet. Most of us willingly allow ourselves to be locked into a very expensive system. It's hard to go against the trend.

There's no one-size-fits-all answer to these questions. We can only answer for ourselves; others are not our responsibility. For ourselves, though, we can look again at what John Wesley has to say on the question of saving.

Wesley felt a responsibility for the money in his care. Most of us don't think that way. The money is ours. But we're all responsible to someone for what we spend. Like John Wesley, I believe we are responsible to God for our possessions and our spending. When we adopt that attitude, our financial priorities change.

The idea of 'stewardship' is well established in the Bible, and Wesley takes up the theme. He talks about how we use our 'talents'. We shouldn't misunderstand this word. Scholars interpret the 'Parable of the Talents' in Matthew's and Luke's Gospels in different ways. Wesley, though, is using 'talent' in its original meaning: an amount of money. Do not throw money away 'in idle expenses', said Wesley.

In particular, we should not waste any part of it 'in procuring the pleasures of sense of whatever kind'. He's not just talking about avoiding 'gluttony and drunkenness', he clarifies. No, he says, 'there is a regular, reputable kind of sensuality, an elegant epicurism'. He's talking about delicate food and fine wines. They do not 'immediately disorder the stomach' nor 'impair the understanding' like over-eating and excessive drinking. Yet they 'cannot be maintained without considerable expense'. Cut it out, he advises, and 'be content with what plain nature requires'.

While I can admire the self-discipline behind Wesley's asceticism, I'm not so sure about this extreme approach. Fine food is a gift to be enjoyed and celebrated. The skill of preparing an excellent meal is a talent (in the modern sense) that can bring pleasure to others. Sharing an enjoyable meal is an aspect of community and fellowship that we should surely relish.

So we don't need to throw out the cookery books or delete the local takeaway's phone number from our contact list quite yet. But this does not mean eating out every week at high-class restaurants or buying the most expensive groceries. Often those practices have more to do with how we want others to see us than with enjoying the food.

Let's keep those expensive restaurants for very special occasions. Last year my wife and I received the most amazing gift from our son and daughter, to celebrate my (significant) birthday. They paid for us to have lunch at Raymond Blanc's *Le Manoir aux Quat'Saisons* near

Oxford. The memorable occasion convinced me that the breathtakingly expensive restaurant deserves its two Michelin stars, but it was even more special because it was literally a once-in-a-lifetime experience. It's a good example of how John Wesley viewed the importance and usefulness of money: our children used what Wesley called 'this precious talent (money)' to give a special gift.

Our everyday reality is different. We certainly eat well - probably better than 98% of the world's population - and my wife is an excellent cook. But we spend money for groceries on basic ingredients. Processed foods, with their hidden sugar and unpronounceable additives, rarely make an appearance.

Those groceries come from the Aldi supermarket, which sells a limited range of high-quality products at fair prices. Several years ago, I would have written 'the unfashionable Aldi supermarket', but consumers increasingly recognise Aldi for efficiency and quality, at prices that are typically 20% lower than so-called mainstream supermarkets. Lidl has a similar reputation.

Over the years, we have saved thousands. We live in Britain, but Aldi are strong in mainland Europe and expanding in the USA. Similar options exist in Canada and Australia. Everyone can save money by seeking out such places, and by strategies like avoiding impulse buying. By shopping for food just once a week, either in person or online, and by using an old-fashioned shopping list, you can avoid costly last-minute visits to convenience stores. By eating meals at regular times, you can avoid snacking on unhealthy and expensive foods. By planning meals, you can stop throwing away a third of the food you buy. Not you? Good, but plenty of people do. By eating out only occasionally, we can save on restaurant bills. And by cutting out or reducing those apparently insignificant everyday expenses for coffee, tea and snacks, we can save a fortune in the long run.

John Wesley also has something to say about 'expensive apparel', 'needless ornaments' and 'superfluous or expensive furniture'. Perhaps I'm wrong in resisting the call to simplicity here, but again I have some difficulty with this. There is much to commend style and beauty for their own sake. Edith Schaeffer's excellent book *Hidden Art*, probably long out of print, is a practical celebration of what a family can do with limited resources to make their home beautiful.[8]

Even so, Wesley had a point. Most of us, both men and women, own more clothes than we could possibly need. And most of us live in homes full of items we haven't used or even seen in the last year. We don't see them, because they are stuffed in a wardrobe, closet or attic. Or hidden in a garage that has no space for a car. For some of us, our home is so full that we have to rent a self-storage unit.

Perhaps the answer lies in our motivation. It can make sense to buy good quality clothes, but if we are buying the brand rather than the quality, so others will see us in fashionable clothes, we need to think again. As to art and furniture, there's nothing intrinsically wrong with appreciating something beautiful, but we don't

---

[8] Edith Schaeffer (1972), *Hidden art*. Wheaton, Ill., Tyndale House.

necessarily have to own it. If we feel we simply must possess that object, then a little self-examination is in order. Possession can become an obsession. Ask yourself whether your aim is 'to gain the admiration or praise of men', as Wesley puts it. His advice is severe: 'do not buy their applause so dear. Rather be content with the honour that cometh from God'.

Wesley is very practical, too, when it comes to spending money on gratifying such desires. You wouldn't lay out a single penny, he suggests, if you realised what 'daily experience shows': that 'the more they are indulged, they increase the more'. 'And would you pay for it, too?', says the sarcastic Wesley. 'What manner of wisdom is this?'

Saving by delaying

'I'm the worst customer for a credit card company because I always pay my balance off every month.' Katie Melua, musician (b. 1984).

In the time you take to read the next paragraph, you could buy a book. Or a shirt. Or a television. Or a car. (Please don't!)

These are opportunities, or problems, that John Wesley could not even imagine, although his father's spell in debtor's prison taught him all about credit. Today, we can buy anything we want in an instant. Even if it's not affordable. Clever advertising presents us with people who look just like us, except that they have found health, beauty, happiness and true love through buying the right shampoo, car or beauty treatment. Are we that stupid? Of course not. But the cleverest - I won't say 'best' - advertising is subliminal. It's the image that sells, not the argument.

And we have to buy NOW! Wait a week, a day or an hour, and it will be too late. Countdown timers show the hours, minutes and seconds until the best deal of the decade expires. The ultimate way to defeat these pressures and temptations is never to use a credit card or any other loan, to pay cash for everything. That may be right for you. Only you can know.

Either way, for every major purchase you need to be clear about how much it's *really* going to cost you. Those monthly payments can be deceptive. When the car salesman asks 'how much per month would you like to pay?', beware. They probably achieve that low monthly payment by extending the period of the loan. Meanwhile, the car is rapidly losing its value. Think instead of the total cost. If possible, plan ahead, save up and pay cash for the car. You'll probably be able to negotiate a healthy discount.

Incidentally, we are sailing in dangerous seas if we visit grocery stores when we're hungry, or any kind of store when we need cheering up. Of course, spending now may make sense if it saves money later. A cool, unemotional calculation may show that the deal really *is* that good.

More probably, you should resist the urge to fulfil your immediate desires and spend income you don't yet have. Some psychologists think the answer is the power of 'delayed gratification', a life skill that is a sign of maturity and supposedly an indicator of future success in life.

The famous 'marshmallow experiment' in the 1960s gave children the choice of eating a marshmallow placed in front of them or leaving it untouched and receiving two marshmallows later. But later research showed that resisting temptation wasn't about iron self-control. Those who put off the pleasure did so by finding better means of gratification, by making the best of their situation. Putting off the pleasure of 'retail therapy' is something we can learn. And it's all the better for the delay.

The trick, though, is not to grit our teeth and bear the pain of waiting, but rather to find a creative way out. As Nick Tasker says, the amazing human mind can find gratification in any situation.

Perhaps you're saving up the deposit for a new apartment, but the latest smartphone has caught your eye. How about buying something small for the apartment instead, or checking out the property pages?

You can still replace your phone if you think you really need to, but research your options. If the cellphone bargain you are being offered has a two-year contract, multiply the monthly payment by 24 and investigate paying a small fraction of the cost by buying a SIM-free phone. Compare iPhones with comparable Android phones from Nokia, for instance. You may be pleasantly surprised.

It's a trivial example, and you can come up with something more relevant to your situation. But you get the idea.

Saving time

'Oh, how precious is time, and how it pains me to see it slide away, while I do so little to any good purpose.'
   David Brainerd (1718-1747).

Time is money.

And time is finite. Like money, it is given to us as a resource that can be used for good or ill. We can choose what we make of the limited 'pot' of months, weeks, days, hours, minutes and seconds at our disposal.

You might disagree. 'There's never enough time', you complain. The pressures of life crowd around us like angry creditors. Children to feed, bosses to satisfy, deadlines to meet. We are 'time-poor'. Everyone has weeks like that. We just have to get through them. Better days may come, but it's hard to believe at that moment.

Often that's the case. But just as often our circumstances present opportunities. This book is an example. Its gestation period was elephantine. I've had the idea in the back of my mind for several years, then other projects took precedence. But the otherwise frustrating coronavirus lockdown has allowed me to focus on writing it.

It is possible to take control.

You might have another objection. 'What does saving time have to do with saving money?' The answer is simple. Freeing up more time gives you the headroom you need to plan properly, cook proper meals, serve others, or even find an additional source of income.

John Wesley had his own strict ideas about the use of time. In 1725, he wrote in his diary his 'General Rules for

Employment of Time', including not devoting too much of it to sleep.

What does that mean to us, residents of the 21st century?

As a boy, I learned the old cliché, 'procrastination is the thief of time'. We didn't have smartphones then; they are today's time thieves. And they are addictive. How often in each day do you check your smartphone or your smart watch? Or should I say every hour? How much time do your teenage children spend on their phones, checking their Facebook, or Instagram, or Snapchat, or TikTok, or Tumblr, or WhatsApp? Or all of them, plus email added for good measure?

I mean none of this to send us all on a guilt trip. Smartphones, personal computers and the internet are in a way just like money and time, to be used for good or ill. We are stewards of these gifts, with the responsibility to make the most positive use of them. But they are at least as difficult to master as money and time, probably much more so, and the three are interconnected.

For most of us, kicking the smartphone and social media habits will free up more time, and probably money too. We may not need to go cold turkey, but we can take practical steps to reduce our dependence.

The actions are easy to describe and hard to implement.[9] It's a little like decluttering your home, which I will look at in the next section. But it's your

---

[9] I'm indebted to David Sawyer's book *Reset* for some of the ideas in this section.

computer and smartphone you will clear out.

First, remove apps you do not use. Second, disable all notifications on your phone and laptop; you don't need the interruptions. Third, remove any social media accounts you can bear to part with (and more if possible); for the ones you keep, only check them at pre-defined intervals, preferably no more than once or twice each day. Fourth, find the night settings on your phone and set them to whatever counts for 'do not disturb' over the night hours. Finally, leave your phone in a separate room, on charge if you like, overnight and when you are 'off duty'.

Perhaps your bosses expect you to be available 24/7. Unless you're a very important on-call emergency worker, you need to educate them. Good luck with that!

Then we come to emails. We need to train our contacts' expectations and our own responses; we don't have to answer every email within minutes of its arrival. Switch off that pesky 'ping' sound that tells you about new messages and set aside certain times of day for dealing with emails.

How many messages are in your inbox right now? 50? 100? 1,000? None? Any of the time management gurus will tell you the best way to master the email monster: 'Inbox Zero'. Each day, you need to get as close as possible to having absolutely nothing in your Inbox folder. You do this by methodically dealing with each message in turn, in one of three ways: respond immediately if you can do so quickly (two minutes is often suggested); defer the task for later, using some task system that means you won't forget it; or delete it.[10] You can also reduce the daily deluge by unsubscribing from as many mailing lists as possible.

I have to admit that I'm not good at email management, but at least I know what I'm trying to achieve.

We may not need to be as strict as John Wesley in using our leisure time, although we can no doubt learn from his sense of focus and commitment. What we can do is make good use of time that would otherwise be wasted. Travel time, whether driving, cycling or on public transport, is one example.

Rather than use the marvellous technology of our smartphone for checking social media, we can listen to podcasts or audiobooks that will improve the mind rather than ensnare it. Safely, of course. The time spent on walking, running and other exercise, too, is an opportunity to listen to something educational. You never stop learning.

These measures will free up more of the time resource. You might use it to spend time with family, to devote to the service of others, or - as many 'financial independence' experts suggest - to earn extra money, balance the budget and retire early. They call these earning opportunities 'side hustles'. But how you use the extra time is up to you.

Time is money.

---

[10] Two people who make their living teaching people how to master these skills are Michael Linenberger (www.michaellinenberger.com) and David Allen (https://gettingthingsdone.com).

Saving simply

'Everything should be made as simple as possible, but not simpler.' Albert Einstein (1879-1955).

In this short section, I look at the whole idea of 'minimalism', meaning that the less we depend on material things, the happier we will be. It makes sense in theory, but it's so hard to put into practice. I must admit that I have not followed this path as far as I should have. Perhaps one day.

I can see the benefits, apart from the obvious cost savings of not buying stuff. The idea itself is easy to grasp. The less we own, the less we have to worry about. John Wesley had little to say about minimalism, but the concept guided his life. He often spoke against accumulating wealth and possessions. And - to use a modern term - he modelled the behaviour.

The modern minimalism movement is about decluttering your life, and the place to start is at home. What are you hoarding?

The recognised world expert on decluttering your house is Marie Kondo from Japan. Her bestselling book *The Life-Changing Magic of Tidying* advocates setting aside several days for a total clear-out.

The book is full of tips on how to go about it, but be warned! Her approach is radical. This is not about stuffing things out of sight. You actually have to get rid. The key is to throw out the things first that offer the most space gained for the least mental stress.

Clothes come first. They take up a lot of space. Some are worn out or no longer in fashion, and they probably hold the least emotional attachment of all our possessions. And we simply own too many of them.

Then come books, documents, cassettes (remember cassettes? I bet you have some stashed away, probably without any means of listening to them), CDs, electronic items, keepsakes, photographs. Leave the items with sentimental value until last. That way discouragement will not stop you in your tracks before you have made progress. You can choose whether to raise a little money for items on eBay or Gumtree, give things away or simply discard them. More on that in the next chapter.

If you can grit your teeth and go through the decluttering process, you will be well on the way to a minimalist lifestyle, possibly with self-sufficiency thrown in. Such thinking was very popular in the 1970s; a BBC television comedy series, *The Good Life*, celebrated the self-sufficiency movement. Interest has waned, but the wisdom of several books of the period has stood the test of time; see the Appendix. Whether or not we adopt minimalism, we can follow the famous advice given by William Morris (1834-1896): 'Have nothing in your house that you do not know to be useful, or believe to be beautiful'.

Saving effectively

Jesus said to them, "Give back to Caesar what is Caesar's and to God what is God's." Mark 12:17 (NIV).

We have already seen how making a sensible financial plan and budget, then monitoring our progress with a simple spreadsheet or personal finance software, can help us be more effective in our saving. I have looked at controlling expenses by cutting out impulse buying and getting a clearer idea of how much things actually cost.

Reducing the burden of debt to zero, apart perhaps from a mortgage on our home, is a priority. The longer you just make the minimum payment, the more your debt is growing.

Gambling and lotteries have not had a mention, but I can dispose of them fairly briskly: 'Don't'.

The one major factor that can scupper our attempts to save money effectively is taxation. Yet tax authorities in most countries provide incentives for saving.

I will move on to investment in the next section, so here we are talking about interest-bearing savings accounts and the like. Current interest rates are woefully low. But they are even lower if you don't take advantage of the tax breaks.

Where to put your savings to minimise tax is confusing, and it would be inappropriate for me to give focused financial advice. Wherever in the world you live, the range of options is mind-boggling. You could employ an advisor; but that's an additional cost.

In the UK, the amount you can currently earn in tax-free interest, under the 'starting rate for savings' and the Personal Savings Allowance, depends on your income. It starts at £5,000 per year and tapers down to zero for the highest earners. You can also save into a Cash Individual Savings Account, or ISA, which is tax-free. Tax treatment for pension saving is even more generous, if that's the right word for Revenue officials.

In the USA, Canada and Australia, tax is no less confusing, but space does not allow more comprehensive detail here. At the end of the book, you will find links to personal finance sites in all four countries. The bottom line, in every sense, is this: keep every dollar or pound you can out of the hands of the Revenue - legitimately.

Saving by investing

'Keep your investment expenses low, for the tyranny of compounding costs can devastate the miracle of compounding returns.' John C. Bogle, businessman (1929-2019).

John Gray was seven years old when his parents upped sticks in Edinburgh, Scotland, in 1849 and moved the family to a new life on a Wisconsin farm. Eight years later, they gave up farming and moved back to city life in Detroit, Michigan.

John Gray (1841-1906), by Clarence Burton (Public Domain)

John joined the family business, at first a toy store and later a candy factory, and prospered. His business enterprises, in lumber, banking and the new science of photography, flourished. He accumulated considerable wealth.

In February 1903, John learned that his young nephew was going into partnership with a friend to build an automobile. They needed investors, preferably people of stature who could draw in others. Gray reluctantly invested $10,500 and received 10.5% equity in the new and unproven company.

The friend's name was Henry Ford. John Gray was one of twelve investors in the Ford Motor Company and became its president. He died suddenly just three years later at 64, but his heirs continued as investors in the company. When the family sold the shares to Henry Ford after the First World War had ended, they had held the investment for 16 years and received over $10 million in dividends. Ford paid them $26 million for their stake. You can do the calculation.

Investment stories like this may make you envious. I hope not. You may hanker after making your fortune in a similar way, but opportunities like that are extremely rare. You are more likely to lose your shirt than make a killing.

Just the same, we can learn from John Gray. Although the Ford Motor Company was profitable within two or three years and his investment soon showed a healthy profit, he and his heirs kept their stake in the company. The long-term approach paid off. Also, he knew the people running the company; he was one of them.

There may be a case for investing in a company if we know the individuals concerned and are confident that the project is sound, or because we have ethical reasons for investing. John Wesley's views on how we earn our living, including not harming others or profiting at their expense, also apply to investment.

The system of stock markets and limited liability companies distances us from the object of our investment. We easily forget that investing is lending to a company, composed of people with aims and objectives that we need to examine. Our own objectives should go beyond 'shareholder value', seen as the gold standard or perhaps the golden calf of much investment advice.

Think differently. Are a company's aims consistent with reducing inequalities, or pollution, or corruption. Do you want to invest in renewable 'green' energy or recycling, in order to play your part in combating climate change? Larger companies will publish their corporate social responsibility policies. But that distance between them and you, created by the market, means that you depend on the publicity penned by their skilful PR people. And how much of that is spin?

I was privileged to visit Albania in the late 1990s, soon after it emerged from Enver Hoxha's repressive Communist regime. Hotels were rare. My two colleagues and I stayed in the apartment of a gently hospitable family, to whom we paid the lavish sum of US $10.00 per person each day, for bed and three excellent meals. Our hosts were thrilled. 'I can invest the $30', said the well-educated, professional man of the house, 'and recoup $100 after a month'. We stared in astonishment. 'That's impossible', we said, 'no investment can be that good'. We could not convince them. They had done it several times, and it had worked perfectly.

The family were victims of the score of pyramid 'investment' scams or 'Ponzi schemes' that boomed in Albania and led to rioting in 1997 when they collapsed. After decades of isolation from the outside world, most of the Albanian population were financially naïve. They were an easy prey. Many of the schemes had government support. When an economic advisor to the prime minister sounded the alarm, he was put in prison.

Today's equivalent is the internet scam. Not all are pyramid schemes, but they become ever more subtle, ever more convincing. Here comes another cliché: 'if it sounds too good to be true, it probably is'.

For most of us, a more conservative approach to investment is appropriate. Investing your money is a fiendishly complex subject. That's why financial experts earn so much. Their fees are just one of the costs that can eat into your investment return. You can pay someone to manage your fund. Or if you fancy your luck as a trader, buying and selling the right companies at exactly the right time, you'll pay charges every time you buy or sell on the stock market. If you hire an advisor or trade aggressively, you'd better be sure the return is good enough to justify it. If you put your money in a managed fund, check out the annual charges.

The right investment decisions for you depend very

much on your stage of life and aspirations. Are you investing for long-term growth? How much risk can you accept? That's why I can't give financial advice to match your personal circumstances, just suggest broad principles. I'm assuming that you are not out to make a quick profit. For most of us, it makes little sense. So the basics apply.

- Investing in the stock market is likely to give the best long-term growth.
- Diversify. A relevant biblical quote is 'Invest in seven ventures, yes, in eight; you do not know what disaster may come upon the land.', (Ecclesiastes 11:2, NIV). I hesitate to challenge the Bible, but today's accepted wisdom is to go a little further. Calculations show that a portfolio of 25-30 stocks spreads the risk adequately.
- Invest in companies you know to be well managed and financially robust, and stick with them (the Warren Buffet approach). The brokerage costs of too many frequent changes soon add up.
- Keep costs down. That might mean investing through a reputable broker that makes your trades in a tax-exempt account without giving advice.[11] For the lowest costs, you could invest in what's called an 'index tracker' fund. These are quite simple, holding shares in a range of companies so that the fund's price rides (up and down) on the back of a reputable

---

[11] Some examples are: Hargreaves Lansdown (UK); Charles Schwab or TD Ameritrade (USA); Questrade (Canada); Bell Direct (Australia).

market index like the FTSE 100, the NASDAQ or the Dow Jones Industrial Average, 'the Dow'. In the long term, a tracker should benefit from the growth of the economy, and the charges are typically low.
- Invest a regular amount and reinvest the dividends. You will reap two benefits that sound technical but aren't: 'dollar cost averaging' and 'compounding'. The first, by ignoring rising and falling prices and not trying to 'game' the market, irons out fluctuations and is often better than trying to buy low and sell high. Actually, the second principle applies both to savings accounts and stock market investments. By reinvesting, you are earning interest on the interest or dividends on the dividends.
- If you do decide to take on higher risk, never invest more than you can afford to lose.

Another way of looking at this is based on direct personal connections. It has biblical precedent. You might call it relational investing.

Economist Dr Paul Mills has worked as a senior policy advisor in the UK Treasury and in the International Monetary Fund. Associated with the Jubilee Centre, a Christian think-tank, Paul has written extensively about relational finance and investment, giving wise suggestions for personal finance.[12] Paul strikes a note of particular

---

[12] Paul Mills, *Investing as a Christian: Reaping where you have not sown* (1996), *The Great Financial Crisis: A biblical diagnosis* (2011), https://www.jubilee-centre.org/cambridge-papers. The biblical Jubilee concept lies beyond the scope of this book. Find out more at the Jubilee Centre website.

concern about the debt-based financial system we now all live with. So - no surprise - his first priority for personal finance is to get out of debt. But he is just as concerned that we should help others clamber out of the credit pit. So, he suggests, consider lending interest-free, especially to relatives. We have an obligation to support our families.

Looking further afield, the line between investment and the savings I considered in the previous section becomes blurred. Paul Mills shows how the banking system insulates us from the individuals to whom we are lending. How can we know what suffering - bankruptcy, repossession, destitution - is being caused in our name? 'We have relinquished the stewardship of our savings to intermediaries', suggests Mills.

Cartoon, The Road to Dividends, by Tad Gorgan, c.1913
(Public Domain, Library of Congress)

What does this mean in practice? How then should we invest? Most important is to free ourselves from the debt trap. Once able to invest, though, to quote Mills directly, we should look closer to home: 'take a stake in a relative's home so that they can minimise their mortgage, or invest in a local or family business to sustain jobs and the local economy'. Should we apply this to our shopping, too?

This resonates with one of John Wesley's central themes: 'we should not "gain all we can" by causing injury to another'. It's a radical approach that few of us try.

Saving by investing in yourself

'An investment in knowledge pays the best interest.'
Benjamin Franklin (1706-1790).

There are two types of investing: the one I looked at in the previous section and another, more subtle one. The first is about stock market investment and retirement accounts like the 401(k) or 403(b) in the USA or SIPPs in the UK. The second relates to investing in yourself. It may sound self-centred, even narcissistic. But hear me out.

You could see saving as investing in yourself financially. But we also need to invest in ourselves spiritually and emotionally. This is where prayer and community come into the picture. But to be of service to our neighbours, near and far, we need to have the skills and physical fitness to be of use to them. Indeed, without those assets we may just be a burden to those around us. Even if we are only considering giving money, our ability to save depends on our earning capacity and in turn on our education, training and fitness. This may mean learning new skills, developing our creative talents or improving our health. The principle of lifelong learning stands in equal importance alongside healthy living.

You don't have to invest vast sums of money in your learning. Many educational books and audiobooks by reputable and knowledgeable authors are free or cost little. And there are thousands of online training courses, workshops and seminars. Many of them are free. All you need is good internet access (isn't that a basic human right today?) and the willingness to devote some time. I'm biased, because the Open University is my alma mater for the MBA, but I recommend OpenLearn, the OU's free learning hub, offering close to 1,000 free courses on almost any subject you can think of. Find out more from the Appendix.

The other area that can help us 'save all we can' is our health. Work-related stress or boredom can lead us to eat the wrong foods, often packed with hidden sugar. And most of us eat far too much. To compound the problem, we spend too much time sitting at a desk, not moving around. When we travel, we climb - or maybe collapse - into the car for even the shortest journeys. Arriving at home, we flop exhausted on to the sofa and watch our favourite TV show, a comforting snack at our side.

Even if we are not clinically obese (as are over 650 million worldwide, more than half of them children), we may be overweight, on the verge of type 2 diabetes without knowing it. Have you checked your Body Mass Index? It's easy.

The solution lies in our hands. With encouragement,

friendly advice (see the Appendix) and a little willpower, you can eat better, take some gentle exercise each day and lose that excess weight. You'll have more energy and feel better about yourself.

Saving your legacy

'If you bungle raising your children, I don't think whatever else you do matters very much.' Jackie Kennedy (1929-1994).

Novelist Anthony Trollope was an investor of time. When he travelled by train on his duties as a Post Office official, he invested the 'dead' time in honing his writing skills. At 34 years of age, he published *The Warden*, the first of his popular Barsetshire Chronicles series. Trollope came up with curious names for his characters. One of my favourites is the Reverend Mr Quiverful, Vicar of Puddingdale and penniless father of twelve children; his wife Letitia constantly struggled to feed them all. The author was no doubt thinking of Psalm 127: 'Children are a heritage from the Lord, offspring a reward from him. ... Blessed is the man whose quiver is full of them.'.[13]

Those of us who are blessed with children, even in smaller quantity, know that you never stop being a parent. It's natural to want to shower them with gifts and to leave them the benefit of our wealth when we are no longer there.

John Wesley took a contrary view. He had no children of his own. Perhaps that made it easier for him

---

[13] Psalm 127:3,5 (NIV).

to tell listeners not to lavish too much money on them. By doing so, he thought, you would be 'purchasing for them ... more foolish and hurtful desires' that will 'pierce them through with more sorrows'. That's not the impression we get as children's faces light up when they receive a present. But perhaps in the long term he is right. As they grow up in our prosperous society, boys and girls are in danger of learning an acquisitiveness that will do them no good in later life. Not to speak of the space taken up by all those quickly forgotten toys.

When Wesley talks of 'parents who think they can never leave their children enough', he is thinking more of grown sons and daughters. I considered the mixed blessing of inheritances in the previous chapter. On this, Wesley is clear. Fairness is less important than character.

'What then would you do', he muses, 'if you was in my case? If you had a considerable fortune to leave?' If he had one child who knew the value of money, he asserts, he would leave that child the bulk of his fortune. To the rest, he would leave enough for them to live in the manner to which they had been accustomed. It may not be fair, but who can argue that it isn't right?

How else should we support our children? Education is crucial, of course. Very few of us can afford private schools, but we can encourage learning at home. For instance, we should teach them by example to deal with money for themselves, starting early. And our responsibility for our family includes whatever insurance we need in place to protect them if we are no longer there. And you have made a will, haven't you? Ultimately, though, the day may come when they take on responsibility for us.

Saving for what?

'If you don't accept failure as a possibility, you don't set high goals, you don't branch out, you don't try - you don't take the risk.' Rosalynn Carter (b. 1927).

If we weren't aware of the need to save at the beginning of this chapter, we are now. But the human mind is a fickle instrument. We need a reason to save, a goal. There's much more chance of sticking at it if there is a clear target. What goals should we set?

For most people, the first priority is to build up an emergency fund for hard times. We read in Proverbs 27:1 (NIV): 'Do not boast about tomorrow, for you do not know what a day may bring.' What if you lose your job? Or you slip and fall, breaking a leg. You need to have enough money tucked away to get you through difficult times. It needs to be easily accessible without delay and enough to see you through a period of recuperation from illness or injury. How much you need will depend on your circumstances and responsibilities. Are you living alone or do you have a family to support? Do you have rent or mortgage payments to keep up? Is anyone else in the family earning? Do you have any other source of income that will keep the family afloat while you are not earning? You may have bought insurance against the more serious risks. Of course we can 'over-insure', just as we can go about in fear of what might happen to us. If an insurance will kick in, how long will the insurers take to pay up?

You will think of other questions you need to consider. Depending on the answers, you should be thinking in terms of an emergency fund between three and nine months' income. Keep it in a simple instant-access savings account. But beware! All that money sitting there can be very tempting.

Some might suggest that this encourages a faithless approach to life. Not at all. There is always a place for prayer and dependence on God. Perhaps someone will miraculously solve your financial problems. But we are to be responsible stewards. We cannot expect a life free of difficulty. Quite the opposite. And if we have resources and the ability to plan, it's not fair to shift our financial burdens on to someone else.

There could be another objection to putting the emergency fund at the top of the priority list. 'I'm deep in debt", you say. 'My credit cards are maxed out.' It's a fair point. Crippling debt is a financial and psychological burden that grows and grows unless you deal with it. But a crippling injury might make matters worse. So your debt situation might make you choose a lower priority for your emergency fund, accepting the greater risk. It's up to you. Take control.

Of course, you might be able to work on both issues at once. Once you have spent time working out your budget, you could set aside twenty percent of your income, half for emergencies, half to drive down your debt.

Once you get these two top priorities under control, you can think about saving for other, more pleasant goals. You will set your own priorities, but children's education, housing, cars and vacations will be on the list, probably in that order.

Increasingly prominent in your thinking will be the question of retirement, especially as you grow older.

Have you heard of the FIRE movement? It stands for Financial Independence Retire Early. The idea is to set financial goals and save enough money so you can leave your boring job in, say, twelve years and live in luxury on a Caribbean island or the Côte d'Azur for the rest of your life. Well, I for one can't think of a more boring prospect. So far I've retired twice, so I suppose I'm in my third career. Who knows, it may not be my last, so the idea of retiring at 45 to a life of leisure leaves me cold.

Yet the FIRE movement does have something to teach us. It's a phenomenon that has taken off in the past three decades, particularly in the United States, since Vicki Robin and Joe Dominguez published *Your Money or Your Life* in 1992. The fundamental idea is to work out how much you will need to save, for how long and through what means, to reach your goal of early retirement at a given age. And then you work hard, possibly seeking additional sources of income. You aim to earn as much as possible and cut back your spending drastically.

Following the FIRE gurus is like a religion. Adherents discuss FIRE calculations; how much capital do you need to survive the rest of your life without working again? They share investment strategies and budgeting triumphs. Taking FIRE seriously means making dramatic sacrifices: cutting back on new clothes, vacations, cars, eating out etc. Frugality is your new way of life.

There's nothing wrong with cutting back now so you can retire early. What matters is what you then do with your time. I suspect most of us would quickly tire of an unproductive life. But early retirement may free us up for a new venture that is very worthwhile. And those later years - emergency fund in place, children flown the nest, mortgage perhaps paid off - may be just the right time to start out on a new path of service.

My former Colorado flying buddy Mark Hyatt retired from the United States Air Force, went into education, retired again but lasted only a year before starting yet another new venture. He built on his love of flying to create Falcon AeroLab (falconaerolab.org). It's a practical technology programme that gives high school students individual tuition in a range of aviation-focused projects and experiences.

The students gain confidence as they learn new skills and knowledge. Numbers have grown in three years from fourteen to over 300. 'I'm having more fun than ever, said Mark, 'but I couldn't have done it if Debbie and I hadn't saved when we were young.'

In the end, if we follow John Wesley's advice and example, the goal of our saving will be both simpler and more challenging.

As Wesley says:

> Let not any man imagine that he has done anything, barely by going thus far, by "gaining and saving all he can," if he were to stop here. All this is nothing, if a man go not forward, if he does not point all this at a farther end. Nor, indeed, can a man properly be said to save anything, if he only

lays it up. ... Not to use, is effectually to throw it away.

We will save more so we can give more, whether out of our surplus now or through our efforts in the future. Ultimately, this is about trust, our attitude to God's sovereignty and our responsibility as stewards.

In the next chapter, I will delve into the 'how to' of giving. John Wesley again: 'When I have money, I get rid of it quickly, lest it find a way into my heart.'

Ideas for Action

- Start to save money, even if the amounts are small e.g. coins tossed into a pot in your kitchen, or your bank's 'small change' account (In the USA, Bank of America has a 'Keep the Change' savings program, in the UK, Nationwide has something similar).
- Decide how much you need in an easily accessible emergency fund, probably three to nine months of income. Set up a regular monthly payment for the day after you receive your salary or other regular income, into the best instant-access savings account you can find.
- If you are burdened with debt, consider matching the 'emergency' deduction 50/50 with an equal payment to reduce your debt. Start with the debts charging the highest interest, unless you are locked in by punitive repayment penalties; for those, you just have to tough it out. Aim for zero debt, apart from your mortgage.
- Make a financial plan and a budget (using a spreadsheet or personal finance app - see the

Appendix).
- Monitor your spending. For one or two months, get an accurate picture of your income and outgoings. Then adjust the plan and budget in the light of experience.
- Emergency fund in place and debt paid off? Time to start saving and giving. Redirect that 'first fruits' monthly payment and don't be afraid to lock the money away for six months or a year; you'll get a better interest rate.
- We need cards, but if credit cards represent too much of a temptation, cut them all up and only use debit cards that take the money straight out of your current or savings account.
- Overhaul your physical fitness. Walk or cycle instead of driving or taking the bus, especially for short distances. Walk up and down escalators, rather than standing still. Exercise safely for 45 minutes at least four days each week: walking, cycling, swimming, sport. If you have health issues, consult your doctor to make sure you stay safe.
- Set a target of walking 1,000 miles this year. It sounds a lot, but it's less than three miles a day.[14] Again, consult your doctor.
- If you are overweight and/or have high blood sugar, transform your eating habits. Check your Body Mass

---

[14] See www.walk1000miles.co.uk.

Index.[15] Set a target weight and follow a low-carbohydrate 'Mediterranean' diet, such as the *8-Week Blood Sugar Diet*. Once again, make sure you take medical advice.

- Invest time and, if necessary, money in your own and your children's learning.
- Don't shop when hungry or thirsty - eat a meal and/or drink water before shopping. Plan ahead and shop weekly, either in person or online. Use a shopping list. Try Aldi, Lidl or the equivalent for your groceries and household needs.
- Compare prices. After a few months, use your financial records to work out how much you are spending. Can you cut back? Buy fewer ready-processed foods. Find simple recipes and learn how to cook using basic ingredients. Think about nutrition: read the small print on the packaging to find out about additives, sugar etc. Are the ingredients really 'basic'?
- Buy for quality and best value, rather than for cheapness.
- Easy decluttering: look around your home for anything you haven't used for a year: books you'll never read again; clothes you've 'grown out of'; foreign currency; old mobile phones. Do you need that ...? Why do you need it? To stay alive? To do your work more effectively? To improve your image? Make the (tiny) effort to find a home for it at a charity

---

[15] See https://www.nhs.uk/live-well/.

- shop or a donation website. It will do somebody good and you'll feel better.
- Harder decluttering: declutter your computer and smartphone: apps, emails, data, email subscriptions.
- Really hard decluttering: Take up Marie Kondo's challenge to declutter your home, in the order: clothes, books, papers, cassettes, CDs, electronic items, keepsakes, photographs and, last of all, sentimental items.
- Every time you buy an item of clothing, give away two or more older items. Every time you buy a book, give one away that you don't think you'll read again.
- Review your shopping. Where do your groceries and other goods come from? Who is paying the price for your low prices? Consider how you can support efforts to improve global justice, perhaps by becoming a customer or supporter of an organisation like Traidcraft in the UK, or in the USA look for the 'Fair Trade Certified™' seal.
- Think about where your skills, knowledge and passions might take you over the next decade.
- Review what you are saving for: housing, children's education, retirement. Set savings goals and protect your savings from taxation, e.g. in a Registered Retirement Savings Plan (Canada), an Individual Retirement Account (USA) or an Individual Savings Account (UK). Australians have fewer tax-free options.
- Watch out for scams!

CHAPTER 4

Give

THERE WAS WISDOM in the order in which John Wesley positioned his advice. First gain, then save, then give. Without the previous chapters, there would be no point in writing this one. Every extra penny gained and saved is one that can be given.

The purpose of all that gaining and saving is not just to build up your wardrobe of clothes and shoes, your hoard of cash, or your portfolio of equities. 'You may as well throw your money into the sea, as bury it in the earth.,' said Wesley. 'And you may as well bury it in the earth, as in your chest, or in the Bank of England. Not to use, is effectually to throw it away.' To make the best use of our money, we need to hold on to it with a loose grip.

In the following pages, I explore the different ways others can gain from the resources we possess. It's not just about money, but that is where we start.

Giving for life

> *'Surplus wealth is a sacred trust which its possessor is bound to administer in his lifetime for the good of the community.'* Andrew Carnegie (1835-1919).

I'm not sure how it is in other countries, but in Britain one of the most dreaded intrusions into life is a tax inspection by Her Majesty's Revenue and Customs. Not so for John Wesley. In 1776, when most British and American eyes were on the Revolutionary War, the tax inspectors came knocking at Wesley's door. In their eyes, he was a rich man. Unlike Andrew Carnegie, though, he had little surplus wealth.

The tax men could estimate Wesley's net worth. His income in one year, mostly from his publications, was more than £1,400 (equivalent to about £250,000 or US$330,000 today), when £30 per year was a good income for a single man. Goods were taxed, rather than income. 'We cannot doubt but you have [silver] plate for which you have hitherto neglected to make an entry', wrote the tax commissioners. Wesley's reply was dismissive: 'I have two silver spoons at London and two at Bristol. This is all the plate I have at present, and I shall not buy any more while so many round me want bread.'[16]

Wesley had developed his attitude to wealth early in life. Once established in the teaching fellowship at Oxford, he soon got used to his comfortable income and thought little about how he was spending it. His view

---

[16] CharlesWhite, *What Wesley Practised and Preached About Money*, Mission Frontiers magazine, September-October 1994.

changed one day after a visit by a poor young girl, whose education he and his 'Holy Club' friends were supporting. He looked at her and said, 'You seem half-starved. Have you nothing to cover you but that thin linen gown?' She replied, 'Sir, this is all I have.' Wesley put his hand in his pocket but found he had spent most of his cash. He was taken aback by his own careless attitude to money. 'Will thy Master say, "Well done, good and faithful steward?", he asked himself, realising he had spent money on 'adorning the walls' that might have 'screened this poor creature from the cold'.[17]

Wesley's approach to the poor and to his own wealth changed from that day. His income at the time was around £30 per year, and he managed to save and give away £2 of it. Years later, he was still living on about £30 per year and giving away hundreds each year. At his death, his estate comprised the coins in his pockets and his collection of books. He had given away everything else. 'I cannot help leaving my books behind me whenever God calls me hence,' he had said.

In later life, Wesley worried that the frugality and diligence he had taught would lead his followers to excessive prosperity and therefore complacency. Looking back in 1789 on the growth of the Methodist movement, he felt its followers had taken on board 'Gain all you can,' some had heeded 'Save all you can,' but few observed 'Give all you can.'

Yet for Wesley the third represented the purpose of

---

[17] *On Dress*, John Wesley, Sermon 88.

the first two. He had a particular concern for the poor. As well as preaching the gospel to them, he befriended them and did what he could for their financial needs, their health and their education. Later in life, he had an influential political voice too. He was an impassioned supporter of anti-slavery campaigns.

In contrast to John Wesley, German theologian and Christian martyr Dietrich Bonhoeffer was not good at saving money or managing his personal finances. He had the cavalier manner of someone who has grown up in a relatively prosperous family. But even if he did not give money a top priority, his views paralleled Wesley's. 'Earthly goods are given to be used, not to be collected,' he wrote.[18] However, his attitude to money can best be described as relaxed and easygoing.

Dietrich Bonhoeffer, c.1939 (Public Domain)

---

[18] Bonhoeffer (1959), p. 194.

Bonhoeffer grew up with few financial cares. But his philosophy went much deeper, and might at first seem contradictory. He was not greatly interested in possessions, but he owned a sports car and rarely hesitated in adding to his extensive collection of books. Yet he lived simply and taught others to do so.

He had a tiny income but was not concerned about receiving a salary, whether as a Christian teacher or, later, as an agent for German Military Intelligence. While in London in 1934, he thought little of spending large sums on international telephone calls. As a result, his parents or his congregation often had to bale him out when his finances got out of hand. He had other things on his mind.

Yet there is much to admire. Less methodical than Wesley, Bonhoeffer was nevertheless known for his careless generosity.

Asked to lead an illegal seminary with no building, no books, and no budget for board and lodging for the ordinands, Bonhoeffer did not hesitate. He donated his own library to the project and threw his life's energy into the cause until it was closed down by the Gestapo in 1937. He bought tickets for the 1936 Olympics out of his own pocket for students who could not afford them. When still young but knowing that his resistance would probably cost him his life, he made a will and gave careful thought to who would inherit his few treasured possessions.

A generous attitude is a good starting point for any of us.

Giving painlessly

'Never turn your back to the poor, for in turning your back to the poor, you are turning it to Christ.' Mother Teresa of Calcutta (1910-1997).

On average, Americans donate around 3% of their income to charitable causes, Australians, Canadians and Brits rather less. Is generosity a skill you can learn? Perhaps not. But it seems to be a habit you can develop. Start small, with easy things.

Each spring, the British charity Stewardship runs a 'generosity challenge' for the 40 days before Easter, the part of the traditional church year known as Lent. The '40acts' campaign transforms what is typically a time for giving up a pleasure into a more positive opportunity to be generous. If you sign up at https://40acts.org.uk, you receive a daily email with a reflection and a challenge to make a difference. The challenges appear within a 'traffic light' system: green is easy, amber is more difficult, red is tough. Over 100,000 people signed up this year.

There are even easier ways to give. Recently, I received a mailing from British charity Traidcraft, one of many organisations in rich countries that work towards just and fair trade for the less prosperous. In the pack was a 'recycling envelope' with a request to send in any unwanted gold, silver or costume jewellery. I had none, but they also suggested sending unwanted currency from any country. I looked in a folder of travel documents from previous trips and discovered cash from Israel, Turkey and Hong Kong, places I may never visit again. Into the envelope it went. I didn't bother to add up how much it was worth, but it probably amounted to about £100 or $130. Cost to me? Ten minutes of my time.

The human heart resists giving, but this often has more to do with inertia than acquisitiveness. We all have a tendency to hoard, to hang on to things we no longer need or want, whether it's money, food, clothes, toys, bicycles or cars. Do you have a garage packed with 'stuff', with no space for a car? Many of us do. Whether in the garage, loft, overflowing cupboards or bursting closets, most of us have things we could live without. Why not give them away? Link it to the decluttering idea in the previous chapter. Win-win. Oh, and by the way, you'll be helping to save the environment too. Win-win-win.

You can of course just carry things round to your local charity shop. But an online option for giving away small items is Ebay; you can sell something and donate all or a percentage of the proceeds to a charity. The buyer is unlikely to be local, so you'll have to pack up and mail the item. You can reasonably expect the buyer to pay the postage, but you need to make the terms clear in your advertisement.

For unwanted large items, the Freecycle network (freecycle.org) is excellent, or will be when it emerges from Covid. Volunteers run over 5,000 local groups worldwide, linking over nine million members. Just find one or more groups near you, sign up, and advertise whatever you want to donate. The world may not beat a path to your door, but the likelihood is that someone local will have been looking for exactly your item and will collect it from your home. Everyone's happy.

More ideas about where to donate things you no longer need are in the Appendix. My wife and I have given away several unwanted items: a sofa and two chairs, a television, a wardrobe, an ottoman, an office chair, a cot and a Bugaboo pram liner.

Giving intentionally

'Money is like manure, of very little use except it be spread.'
Francis Bacon (1561–1626).

Just as we plan our savings, so too can we plan our generosity. To connect with the 'start easy to get the generosity habit' idea of the previous section, it can be as simple as setting up a (large!) jam jar in the kitchen and dropping in those coins that are weighing down pockets or purses. Or you can be more determined: drop in the amount you would have spent on coffee one day each week. Or every day.

Even that won't get us far in the generosity stakes, though. A more ambitious level of intentionality is to pick up the 'first fruits' idea from Saving and apply it to Giving. Set up a 10% deduction - the biblical tithe - the day after payday to your church, a charity of your choice or a general charity fund such as Charities Aid Foundation in Britain or Fidelity Charitable in the USA. (Other suggestions are in the Appendix.) Such a fund saves tax, of course, and you can later donate from it to the charity that most needs your support.

Many employers will set up a tax-free deduction from your salary. In Britain it's called Give as You Earn. If you think you can spare 20%, try that. Even at 10%, you'll be far exceeding the charitable giving of the average American, Canadian, Australian or Brit.

The first advantage of this regular 'payday' giving is practical, exactly the same as with regular saving. You are setting the money aside before you can spend it. But with giving there is much more to it than that. You are holding the resources put under your care with a loose grip. You recognise that your task is to act as an accountable steward of those resources. You are committing yourself to putting your giving first, ahead of your other 'needs'. I believe God will honour that commitment. Try it and see.

You don't need to make a big noise about your donations. There's a lot to be said for giving secretly, not letting your left hand know what your right hand is doing. (The *Secret Millionaire* television series springs to mind, but perhaps it's not such an outstanding example. There's nothing very secret about being filmed while you give money away.) On the other hand, we need to balance against that the benefits of building a relationship with the recipient charity: we will be better informed and more able to target our giving. Be strategic.

Giving strategically

> *'Nobody made a greater mistake than he who did nothing because he could do only a little.'*
> Edmund Burke (1729-1797).

> *'Don't judge each day by the harvest you reap but by the seeds that you plant.'* Robert Louis Stevenson (1850-1894).

'Captain Sir Tom' became one of the great heroes of the Covid-19 pandemic in Britain, during the bizarre coronavirus year of 2020. Captain Thomas Moore was a

99-year-old Yorkshire-born veteran of the Second World War. In April 2020, he decided to do something to support those he saw as genuine heroes: the men and women of the National Health Service. They were battling Covid-19, keeping patients alive with limited resources.

Tom Moore during WW2 (Public Domain)

At 99, Tom couldn't run a marathon. He couldn't sail across the Atlantic. But in his time he had served his country in Sumatra, India and Burma. He had raced motorcycles after the war. He did not lack courage. In April 2020, Tom decided to walk laps of his garden, with the help of a walking frame, and raise money for NHS charities. With luck, he might raise £1,000 ($1,300) from family and friends by his hundredth birthday, three weeks away on 30th April.

He did better than that. The story spread around the country and struck a chord with many who until then had not heard his name. He became a national celebrity, interviewed for television and newspapers.

By the time Tom reached his 100th birthday, more than 1.5 million people had donated. His 'big day' was rather bigger than he had expected. The amount donated had risen to a staggering £32 million ($40 million). He received 150,000 birthday cards, as soldiers mounted a guard of honour for his hundredth 25-yard lap of the garden. A Spitfire and Hurricane of the Royal Air Force's Battle of Britain Memorial Flight flew past. To mark the day more permanently, he was promoted to honorary colonel.

Three months later, on 17th July, HM the Queen invited Tom to Windsor Castle. She conferred a knighthood on him in her first public engagement since lockdown: he became Colonel Sir Thomas Moore. I'm no fan of celebrity culture. But Colonel Sir Tom - with at last count two honorary doctorates and with buses, trains, gardens, police dogs, horses and powerboats named after him - is one to celebrate. Perhaps we can't all achieve as much as Tom, but we can emulate his example. Many have done so.

This is strategic giving: to donate time, effort or money in a way that inspires others or unlocks other donations. Often we cannot know at the outset what the impact will be. Tom didn't. It's an act of faith. But we can set up the process to gain support, make the effort, and pray that our venture will be supported. One simple and popular way to do this is through sponsored running, walking, parachuting, knitting - you name it - raising support through a website like Justgiving. The more leverage you can achieve, the better.

Of course, donating your time has value in itself. The Cotswold village of Bledington, close to where we live, had a pub, a church and little else. A group of residents worked together for three years to gain land, grants and donations to fulfil their dream: to build a community shop and cafe. Today, volunteers donate their time to serve groceries, coffee and snacks. Although we don't live in the village, my wife was one of them. The struggle to open the shop and keep it going has been far from easy. But, although the people of Bledington couldn't have known it, their timing was perfect. The shop quickly became a critical lifeline for isolated villagers locked down by the coronavirus pandemic. You never know what impact you can achieve.

Also strategic is to watch out for opportunities to have your donation matched. Each year in December, for example, a group of philanthropists get together and offer to match donations to selected charities one-for-one. It's called The Big Give.

Leveraging is also an outcome of lending your money rather than giving it. We have already seen from Paul Mills how lending to family and local businesses is a thousand times more relational than lending through a bank.

We can look further afield too. At its best, the practice of microfinance, providing small loans to those who would otherwise not get credit, has helped to bring millions out of poverty. Since being pioneered by Muhammad Yunus in Bangladesh in the 1970s, the idea has sometimes been hijacked by the unscrupulous. You need to be sure you are working through a reputable non-profit organization. But through lending money in this way you are supporting your 'neighbour' on the other side of the world.

Giving to neighbours

'Those who give to the poor will lack nothing, but those who close their eyes to them receive many curses.' Proverbs 28:27 (NIV).

It's an age-old question: who is our neighbour? In the parable of the Good Samaritan told by Jesus, the Samaritan is the foreigner, the hated outsider. Yet he is the one who comes to the rescue of an injured man whom thieves have attacked. Others, respected pillars of society, look away and avoid contact with the victim.

How do we make sense of this story in our 21st century world of instant global communication, where virulent pandemics affect the disadvantaged all over the planet? Overwhelming needs bombard us from around the globe, too many needs. Television and social media bring much more to our attention than simply discovering a victim at the roadside. Sometimes the messengers' motives and accuracy are not trustworthy. Often, we learn of problems through heart-rending images, perhaps carefully crafted by professional fundraisers. Everyone needs our money, from the impassioned televangelist to the disaster relief agency. We feel powerless. What can we do?

The Samaritan can teach us some lessons. First, he helps the victim because he happens to be passing by. He does not seek the situation, but when it comes before his face, he does what he can. Second, he does not try to solve the problem alone. He leaves money with the innkeeper. Third, he thinks about the victim's long-term needs and acts strategically. Finally, he cannot solve the entire problem; he does what he can.

Trying to take on all the needs of the world will quickly overwhelm us. We will give up in despair. But that does not mean doing nothing. We can work on the issues that present themselves to us, where we can add value. Global justice is one of those issues. I have mentioned Traidcraft, the pioneers of Fair Trade in Britain. My wife and I have supported the organisation since its foundation in 1979, mostly through buying foodstuffs and other goods that we know have been fairly traded.

It's possible to get involved more directly. Some years ago, we visited Arequipa, Peru, and got to know Barry and Anthea Harrison, a missionary couple from Belfast who were working there. Their love for the Peruvian poor was obvious. 'Our knitting groups need an outlet,' they explained. 'They produce beautiful alpaca knitwear, but they don't have a market for it.'

'Send it to us,' we replied, 'and we'll see what we can do.' Soon after we got home, a massive carton arrived from Arequipa. You can pack plenty of sweaters into a big box. We transferred the money to the Harrisons, held 'alpaca parties' in our home, and sold the sweaters at cost. Several similar shipments followed. Admittedly, it wasn't much of a dent in the problem of global inequity.

We never 'scaled up', but the Peruvian knitters later got an outlet in Britain through Traidcraft. Our contribution was tiny, but we were able to tackle a problem that presented itself.

Giving to the future

'Only when the last tree has died and the last river been poisoned and the last fish been caught will we realise we cannot eat money.' Native American Proverb.

How our giving - of time, effort or money - contributes to the future we leave for our children and grandchildren has become more acute in the past half-century. Fifty years have passed since Milton Friedman disdainfully challenged the idea that:

> business is not concerned "merely" with profit but also with promoting desirable "social" ends,' that it should take seriously its responsibilities for providing employment, eliminating discrimination, avoiding pollution and whatever else may be the catchwords of the contemporary crop of reformers.

Such 'nonsense,' he wrote, 'does clearly harm the foundations of a free society,' within which 'there is one and only one social responsibility of business—to use its resources and engage in activities designed to increase its profits so long as it stays within the rules of the game.'[19]

This is another area where the distinction between giving, saving and investment becomes hazy, and in the previous chapter I mentioned the need to go beyond 'shareholder value' when investing. In an atmosphere of post-truth politics and climate change denial, it is difficult to know the facts about anything. Yet one fact is undeniable: we humans are causing irreparable damage in a hundred ways to the world for which we should be stewards and guardians.

My friend Chip Hauss drew my attention to a movement in business that recognises climate and other areas in which the profit motive is harmful. According to the 'Imperative 21' coalition,[20] the time has come to shift the focus from the shareholder to the stakeholder, understood in the broadest sense. This business-led network represents over 70,000 companies with the ambitious aim of re-shaping capitalism 'to create shared wellbeing on a healthy planet.' The leaders claim that a powerful business case exists for re-imagining business, by designing for future interdependence, investing for justice and changing accounting practice to include the interests of all stakeholders: that means customers, suppliers, employees and later generations as well as those who own the business.

For those of us living in countries where the Christian

---

[19] *The Social Responsibility Of Business Is to Increase Its Profits*, Milton Friedman, 13 September 1970, The New York Times Archives.

[20] https://www.imperative21.co.

faith is embroiled in bitterly divisive politics, it is too easy to dismiss such ideas as 'radical socialism'. Battle lines are drawn. We should at least be willing to listen and consider what stewardship means to where we work, how we save and invest, and the destination for our charitable giving.

Giving a real legacy

The two most powerful warriors are patience and time.' Leo Tolstoy (1828-1910).

Back in the early 1970s, I flew in a C-130 Hercules aircraft from Khartoum, Sudan, to Juba, in the southern part of what was then one country. Sudan was at the time enjoying a pause of several years between its first and second civil wars. During the short stopover, I noticed a gleaming white Cessna of Mission Aviation Fellowship parked on the tarmac. Now, MAF is an organisation that I had been supporting since my teenage years when I started my own flying career. It's a Christian 'airline' providing transport to missionaries, relief workers and development organisations. The British MAF works alongside its American and Australian counterparts, but itself concentrates mostly on Africa.

As I had time in hand, I wandered over to talk to the pilots. This was a golden opportunity to meet some MAF people in the field. I'm not sure, but one of the men with whom I was chatting may have been Stuart King. Stuart had been instrumental in founding MAF UK. He recently passed away, just as I was pondering this section of the book. It started me thinking about legacies.

Most of us think of legacies as an amount of money left

in a will. And that is important. We know as we prepare our wills (you have made a will, haven't you?), that any lifetime commitments to supporting our family have become less important. Actually, it's amazing how many of us avoid making a will. Death is something we'd prefer not to think about.

None of us knows when we will die. As we get older, though, our children may become less dependent on us. It may be time to revisit our financial planning, with the freedom to be more generous with our money. After we've gone, we can no longer spend it. You have updated your will, haven't you?

When you plan how others will dispose of your assets after death, it doesn't have to be complicated. You just need to consider those you leave behind, for whom you are responsible, and provide adequately for them. We saw in Chapter Two, though, that we may not be doing our children any favours by leaving them a large inheritance; it can be a mixed blessing. The centuries resound with stories of young men and women who have gone off the rails because their inherited wealth allowed them to do anything they wanted.

When we have provided appropriately for family, we may have capacity to make our 'wealth' - however modest it might be - do a lot of good. We won't need it any more.

You can leave money to an individual, but you can also leave a legacy to a non-profit organization. In British tax law, a legacy to a charity is exempt from inheritance tax, and similar rules apply in other tax regimes. You might use charitable legacies to reduce how much of your estate goes to the government. Perhaps there are charities you would like to have supported more during your lifetime. This is your chance to redress the balance. Charities are aware of this, of course, and encourage supporters to make a legacy. Some will help you make your will. The larger ones even have legacy departments.

But there's a different type of legacy, the kind that started me thinking about Stuart King. I have absolutely no idea about Stuart's financial situation. I don't have a clue how much money he had during his lifetime. I suspect that, being a missionary, he never had much surplus cash to splash around. He probably depended on donations to support him and his family. But Stuart left a very substantial legacy. At the end of his 98-year life, he could look back on a remarkable achievement. He had helped make it possible for relief workers and missionaries to travel quickly and safely in remote and hostile locations.

Stuart was a committed Christian who left the Royal Air Force at the end of the Second World War. He joined two others in harnessing their shared passion - flying - to support missionaries in remote areas. Mission Aviation Fellowship was the result. With another former RAF officer, Stuart flew from Britain to Africa in 1948, covering 4,000 miles in a small twin-engine Miles Gemini aircraft.

During their viability survey of East Africa, the Gemini crashed in Burundi. Stuart and his colleague survived, returning with tails between legs to Britain and a sceptical mission board. Eventually, they persuaded their backers to let them set up an MAF operation in Sudan. Based in Khartoum, they operated light aircraft throughout the country, but particularly in the south, where the need for aviation support seemed greatest. Stuart later based himself in southern Sudan and laid the foundation for mission aviation, not just there but in many parts of Africa and the rest of the world. He later moved on to lead MAF UK as its general director. Stuart King sacrificed the potential for a lucrative career in military or civil aviation to fulfil a mission to which he felt called. The results were astounding.

MAF today aims to 'transform the lives of the world's most isolated people' through aviation. From tiny beginnings, an international partnership has grown. It serves organisations like the United Nations Development Programme, the World Health Organisation, World Vision, Tear Fund and the Red Cross. It flies to over 1,000 locations in two dozen developing countries. All of this grew from the vision, determination, and commitment of a few people, among them Stuart King.

That's a legacy.

Giving radically

> *'Love seeks one thing only: the good of the one loved.'*
> *Thomas Merton (1915-1968).*

Nicky Gumbel of London's megachurch, Holy Trinity Brompton, tells the story of a young boy who was asked to donate blood to his sister.[21] She was seriously ill, but he had already recovered from the same disease and had developed antibodies. After the doctor's explanation, the five-year-old bravely agreed to donate his blood. As he watched his sister recover during the transfusion, the child betrayed a misunderstanding of the implications of his selfless decision. He thought he would have to give all his blood. With a slight tremor in his voice, he asked 'Will I start to die right away?'.

Gumbel draws an important theological lesson from the story. Here, we can just admire the courage.

Our sacrifice may not be as radical. Provided you are healthy and reasonably young, you can help others by giving blood or by allowing your organs to benefit a sick person after your death. In Britain, your consent to be an organ donor is assumed unless you have registered an opt-out, although doctors will consult your surviving relatives.

Any discussion of death may seem morbid. We avoid it. It's the great taboo. Like making a will, though, planning for your inevitable departure is a last gift for your family.

Giving expectantly

'They travel lightly whom God's grace carries.' Thomas à Kempis (c. 1379-1471).

I have to admit that this is a difficult section for me to write. I can't claim to have put the ideas I'm going to

---

[21] Nicky Gumbel (2018), *Bible in One Year*, Day 115.

describe here into practice in any meaningful way. But it would be remiss of me not to include them in this book.

Ryan Thomas Holladay served as the lead pastor of Lower Manhattan Community Church in New York City for a decade before moving with his family to Rwanda. In his book *You of Little Faith*, Holladay advocates extravagant, aggressive giving. Surprisingly, he is not talking about selflessness. Instead, he means what he calls 'faith-based giving: when you give a large (and ever-increasing) percentage of your income to God because you want something from him in return.'[22]

In the book, Ryan tells the story of how he and his wife committed to giving away a large proportion of their income, starting with 10% but rapidly rising. Long story short: they found their giving unlocked blessings over and above what they had given, but in ways they had not expected. Easy to say, 'Aha, that's just the church trying to get hold of people's money.' We have heard of televangelists who promise that God will repay you tenfold if you just donate - probably to help them keep their 'essential' private jet. Holladay's message seems to teeter on the edge of the 'prosperity gospel.' We should beware!

That would be unfair. When Ryan suggests we suffer because we don't give enough, he has 'walked the talk' himself with his family. Also, he has encouraged his church to give; at the time of his writing, they were giving

---

[22] Ryan Thomas Holladay (2019), *You of little faith: how bold giving leads to great blessing*. Grand Rapids, Michigan, Baker Books.

away one-third of their income - and rising. And another thing: a charlatan doesn't pack up and move with his family to Rwanda. Just the same, the argument seems too 'transactional' and doesn't seem to allow much room for God's grace.

There are parallels with what we have learnt from John Wesley, both about the significance of money and the crucial importance of committing it to God. And because money is so important to us, Holladay suggests, 'giving is the perfect test of faith.' As I say, this section is difficult to write; I can't claim direct personal experience. Read Holladay's book. You decide.

Another book that takes a similar, if less radical, line is *Renewing your Money Mind*.[23] In it, Barbara Galloway gives plenty of practical advice on budgeting, debt, spending, saving and investing, but she also suggests that we need to change our mindset. 'To keep money,' she writes, 'you must let go of your love for it; your desire for it; your worship of it; your seeking it at all costs; and its hold on you.' That's not so different from Holladay's viewpoint, or Wesley's.

Ideas for Action

- Just as for saving, build up your giving habit from small beginnings. Give away things you no longer need: old mobile phones (don't forget to remove your SIM and memory cards and perform a factory reset),

---

[23] Barbara R Galloway (2020), Renewing Your Money Mind: How to Go from Common Cents to Kingdom Wealth, Christian Faith Publishing.

- unwanted clothes, books, ornaments, etc.
- Alongside your budget for debt reduction (if needed), set up regular monthly payments to a tax-free charity account, your church and/or other charities. Don't make a song and dance about it; keep it quiet.
- If you are money-poor but time-rich, think about where you could add value by volunteering or offering hospitality in your home. 'Donate' your time to leverage donations by others: sponsored marathon running, walking, weight loss, etc.
- Next February, sign up at *https://40acts.org.uk* to participate in the *40acts* Lent generosity challenge.
- When you give, think of your poor and needy neighbours: locally and on the other side of the globe, especially those who have been more severely affected by the coronavirus pandemic. Transform that thought into concrete action.
- Make a will. It doesn't have to be complicated or expensive, and it gives you the opportunity to give more generously than is possible during your time on earth.
- Think laterally about your legacy and that of your family. What can you do that your children and grandchildren will be proud of? What have your parents and grandparents done that you could capture in print, an audio recording or a video, before it is lost?
- Finally, consider the call to radical and expectant giving with which this chapter ended.

CHAPTER 5

Bringing it all together

HAVING LOOKED IN DETAIL at gaining, saving and giving, we can briefly examine how John Wesley's advice might apply to us as we progress through our hectic lives.

Stages of Life

> 'It was the best of times, it was the worst of times.' Charles Dickens (1812-1870), A Tale of Two Cities.

To quote Wesley:

> Do all the good you can, by all the means you can, in all the ways you can, in all the places you can, at all the times you can, to all the people you can, as long as ever you can.
>
> Money is one of the most important tools we have for

doing the right thing. Whatever stage of life we have reached, in good times and in bad, we can apply John Wesley's advice: gain all you can, save all you can, then give all you can. But how we apply it depends on our age and circumstances.

Young, single, fancy-free

'Good habits formed at youth make all the difference,'
Aristotle (384-322 BC).

Our youth is the time to establish financial patterns that, if fixed in our minds and daily routines, can persist for decades. Here parents can help children to learn habits of earning pocket money, saving prudently and giving generously. It's never too soon.

But then, all too soon, they grow up and leave home. The temptations of modernity materialise. As college or university students, young men and women are in a strange financial situation: inexperienced but managing their own money; confident but vulnerable; more or less penniless, but potentially high earners. They are rich pickings for bankers with long-term horizons, competing for their business. In the first weeks, enticing offers of low-cost credit appear.

A few years pass. Now a young professional, you are frantically busy. There's no time to plan, to budget, to save, to give. Unless those early habits are securely rooted, they may be forgotten. The rushed visit to the coffee shop or bar wins hands-down over the half-hour with a personal finance spreadsheet. There are quite enough spreadsheets in the office, thank you.

More years go by. Relationships develop. Perhaps you are thinking of marriage. It's a partnership financially as well as in many other ways. That hard-won financial independence is suddenly under threat. You are yoked to a person with a different upbringing, different habits, different expectations. Decisions and responsibility have to be shared. Welcome to marriage.

Young couple, 1.9 children

'Now listen, you who say, "Today or tomorrow we will go to this or that city, spend a year there, carry on business and make money." Why, you do not even know what will happen tomorrow. What is your life? You are a mist that appears for a little while and then vanishes'. James 4: 13-14 (NIV).

Time is moving on. You are finding your feet. The family has money coming in. But you have responsibilities: children in expensive schools, higher costs on the way. You and your spouse don't always agree about money. Why can't we afford our dream home? How can we replace the ageing car?

You need both incomes to keep the ship afloat. You manage to donate to church and charities - most months - but credit cards are maxed out.

It can't go on like this. Time to take stock.

Middle-aged and prosperous

'Knowledge is proud that he has learned so much; wisdom is humble that he knows no more.' William Cowper (1731-1800).

You have a couple of decades of working life behind you. Established in your career, you are proud of your attainments. You have worked so hard.

Over the years, spousal misunderstandings about money have been ironed out. Children have left home for university, but they are no less dependent.

You may not be a millionaire, but you are at last learning some habits of financial success, such as living beneath your means.

Maybe it's time to rediscover the untapped creativity of your youth. Some say that people achieve peak creativity in their thirties and forties. And we never stop learning.

Senior and free again

'Only a life lived in the service to others is worth living.'
Albert Einstein (1879-1955).

There is an old English proverb, 'the older the fiddle, the sweeter the tune.' I'm no musician, but I can understand the beauty of a Stradivarius.

Assuming that you practised good financial management earlier in life, you will have made reasonable provision for retirement. Much of the financial pressure is off.

One never stops being a parent, but the responsibility to support your children financially is behind you. Your children have children.

At 98, Titian created a masterly painting of the Battle of Lepanto. Old age can be a time of great fruitfulness. It may present an opportunity to set off in a new direction. Financial decisions may be a matter of choice rather than necessity. This could be your chance to support the younger generations in a fresh way: loans for housing, education for grandchildren.

It was President Jimmy Carter who declared that his 22 grandchildren and great-grandchildren kept him young.

Summing up

> 'On some positions, Cowardice asks the question, "Is it safe?" Expediency asks the question, "Is it politic?" And Vanity comes along and asks the question, "Is it popular?" But Conscience asks the question, "Is it right?".' Martin Luther King, Jr (1929-1968).

The breakneck gallop through the generations that we have just experienced could only hit the highlights. It was a series of snapshots, caricatures even. The issues that face us in the various phases of life differ, but John Wesley's principles stay the same.

I hope the preceding chapters have opened up their relevance to us today.

I promised at the outset that this would not be a 'Make your Millions' book, nor would I be trying to 'upsell' a personal finance course. I also said that I would write the book from a Christian viewpoint, but hoped that those of other faiths or none would find it of value. That remains the case. So when I say that a key aspect of 'gaining, saving and giving' is prayer, you can decide for yourself how to interpret it. Let me just say that a confidence that God is in control is a thread that runs through every part of this book.

The prophet Jeremiah, not noted for his cheerfulness, firmly believed in God's sovereignty. His dire warnings to the people of Israel were followed by reassurance that God would rescue them in the end. He used the powerful metaphor of God as a potter, with the people representing the clay pots being formed. On its own, the picture suggests too passive a role for us. In fact, we are on the case too. The apostle Paul uses the image of the potter in his letter to the Romans. But when writing to the believers at Philippi he emphasises the need for them to be active too, as God works in them towards the purpose he has for their future (Philippians 2:12-13). And by the way, they shouldn't grumble.

The last word

> *'The rich are wise in their own eyes; one who is poor and discerning sees how deluded they are.'*
> *Proverbs 28.11 (NIV).*

Let's give the last word to the man who inspired this book. He gained, saved and gave. He challenges us, centuries later, to do the same.

In updated language, this is what John Wesley wrote at the end of his sermon on money:

> If you are still in doubt, put these questions as statements to God in prayer: "Lord, you see that I am going to spend this money on ... and you know that I am acting as your trusted steward according to your design." If you can make this prayer with a good conscience then you will know that your expense is right and good.
>
> These, then, are the simple rules for the right use of money. Gain all you can, without bringing harm to yourself or neighbour. Save all you can by avoiding waste and unnecessary luxuries.

> Finally, give all you can. Do not limit yourself to a proportion. Do not give God a tenth or even half what he already owns, but give all that is his by using your wealth to preserve yourself and family, the Church of God and the rest of humanity. In this way you will be able to give a good account of your stewardship when the Lord comes with all his saints.
>
> I plead with you in the name of the Lord Jesus, no more delay! Whatever task is before you, do it with all your strength. No more waste or luxury or envy. Use whatever God has loaned to you to do good to your fellow Christians and to all people. Give all that you have, as well as all that you are, to him who did not even withhold his own Son for your sake.[24]

Myself, I can't claim ever to have done this consistently. Just the same, I hope that the previous chapters have given you food for thought. I have learnt a lot as I tried to restate Wesley's eighteenth-century doctrine in modern terms and shared ideas on how to put them into practice. May each of us be encouraged on our journey towards following his example.

**

Thank you for reading
Gain Save Give
I hope you have found it of interest and value. Please take a few minutes to leave an honest review wherever you purchased it. For Amazon, follow these links:

USA: *https://bit.ly/GSGreviewUSA*

---

[24] By Richard Hall, (*Creative Commons License: Attribution Share Alike*).

UK:	https://bit.ly/GSGreviewUK
Canada:	https://bit.ly/GSGreviewCA
Australia:	https://bit.ly/GSGreviewAUS

Thank you!

I will also be delighted to receive any individual comments by email to peter@cloudshillpress.com.

****

Also by Peter Dixon

A work of extraordinary relevance in today's troubled and volatile times', Lord (Richard) Dannatt, former head of the British Army.

Find out more at https://bit.ly/DixonPeacemkrs

Acknowledgments

During this strange year, the Covid-19 pandemic has been at the centre of everyone's life, including mine. This has been my second 'lockdown book'. All research has been online, all communications remote or at best two metres distant.

Details about John Wesley's life and ministry are mostly gleaned from Roy Hattersley's comprehensive, objective and often critical biography *John Wesley: a brand from the burning*, but only direct quotes are cited in a footnote. Direct quotes from Wesley himself are primarily taken from his sermon *The Use of Money*. The updated version of the sermon is by Richard Hall, a Methodist minister in Shropshire, England, and is reproduced under the *Creative Commons License: Attribution Share Alike*. I am grateful to Bonhoeffer historian Rev Dr John McCabe for his insight on Dietrich Bonhoeffer's attitude to money.

Many individuals have generously given their valuable time to read drafts, and rescued me from my mistakes and oversights. They include Richard Paice of the Worshipful

Company of Pattenmakers, Revd Martin Short of St Edward's, Stow-on-the-Wold, Dr Tim Demy, former British Army chaplain Revd Graham Hadfield, and Colonel Mark Hyatt.

I am grateful to all.

As ever, my family have supported my efforts, encouraging progress and commenting on ideas. My wife Ingrid, in particular, set to work with her meticulous eye for detail and helped polish the final product.

Any residual errors are my own.

APPENDIX

Resources

Web resources

Note: Inclusion of resources in these lists, provided in good faith, does not imply endorsement of any product or service.

Personal Finance Facilities and Advice

UK

https://www.moneyadviceservice.org.uk, personal finance advice.
https://moneysavingexpert.com (Martin Lewis), personal finance advice.
https://www.ft.com/personal-finance, personal finance advice.
Hargreaves Lansdown, *https://www.hl.co.uk/*, online broker.

USA

https://money.usnews.com/money/personal-finance, personal finance advice.
https://www.msn.com/en-us/money/personalfinance, personal finance advice.
https://christianpf.com/the-best-christian-financial-websites/, links to Christian personal finance websites and blogs.
https://www.investopedia.com/personal-finance-4427760, personal finance advice.
https://www.thebalance.com/, personal finance advice.
https://usatoday.com/money/personal-finance/, personal finance advice.
Charles Schwab https://www.schwab.com/, online broker.
TD Ameritrade https://www.tdameritrade.com, online broker.

Canada

https://www.canada.ca/en/services/finance.html, personal finance advice.
https://www.practicalmoneyskills.ca/personalfinance/, personal finance advice.
My Money Coach https://www.mymoneycoach.ca/, personal finance advice.
https://youngandthrifty.ca/, personal finance advice.
https://www.moneysense.ca/, personal finance advice.
https://www.theglobeandmail.com/investing/personal-finance/, personal finance advice.
Questrade https://www.questrade.com, online broker.

Australia

https://www.choice.com.au/money/, personal finance advice.
https://moneysmart.gov.au/financial-advice, personal finance advice.
Bell Direct *https://www.belldirect.com.au*, online broker.

Debt support

USA

Dealing with Debt *https://www.usa.gov/debt*, federal government information on debt.
National Foundation for Credit Counseling https://www.nfcc.org, non-profit organization offering debt counselling.

Canada

https://www.canada.ca/en/financial-consumer-agency/services/debt/debt-help.html, government advice and warnings about debt counselling.
My Money Coach/Debt
https://www.mymoneycoach.ca/blog/christian-credit-debt-financial-counselling-consolidation-services-canada, advice on debt counselling.

Australia

https://www.servicesaustralia.gov.au/individuals/subjects/manage-your-money/deal-debt, government advice on dealing with debt.

Christians against Poverty Australia, *https://capaust.org/*, Christian debt support.

UK

Christians against Poverty *https://capuk.org/*, charity started by Bradford man John Kirkby in 1996, helping people get out of debt.
Money Saving Expert/Debt *https://www.moneysavingexpert.com/loans/debt-help-plan/*, offering a plan to get out of debt.
National Debtline, *https://www.gov.uk/national-debtline*, confidential government call line (0808 808 4000) giving debt advice.

Charitable giving

International

freecycle.org, international network for free items.
eBay.com, *eBay.co.uk*, post items for sale, donate proceeds to charity.

UK

https://account.greenredeem.co.uk/greener-living/lifestyle/charities-raising-money-from-recycling---and-how-you-can-help, advice on 'green' giving.
Stewardship *stewardship.org.uk*, advice and facilities for philanthropy, including tax-free charity account.
The Big Give, *donate.thebiggive.org.uk*, matched funding campaign in December for selected charities.
JustGiving *justgiving.com*, platform for sponsored

fundraising projects.
Charities Aid Foundation *https://www.cafonline.org/*, advice and facilities for philanthropy, including tax-free charity account.
40 Acts *https://40acts.org.uk*, 40-day Lent generosity challenge, starting in February each year.
http://www.recycle4charity.co.uk, recycle printer ink cartridges.
https://www.recyclenow.com/, general recycling advice.

Australia

Philanthropy Australia *https://www.philanthropy.org.au/*, general information about Australian charitable giving.
Australian Philanthropic Services *https://australianphilanthropicservices.com.au/*, sets up and administers tax-efficient 'private ancillary funds'.
The Good Cause Company *https://www.thegoodcause.co*, information about Australian charities.

USA

https://www.usa.gov/donate-to-charity, government tax advice on charitable donations.
CAF, America *https://www.cafamerica.org*, facilitates tax-efficient giving in the USA and internationally.
Charity Navigator *https://www.charitynavigator.org*, ratings for charities.
Fidelity Charitable *https://www.fidelitycharitable.org/*, 'donor-advised' charitable fund
https://electronics.howstuffworks.com/donate-cell-phone-charity.htm, donating old cellphones.

Canada

https://www.canada.ca/en/services/taxes/charities.html, government tax advice on charitable donations and taxation.

Canada Helps *https://www.canadahelps.org/en/*, fundraising portal.

Charity Intelligence *https://charityintelligence.ca/*, research on charities.

Health

UK

https://www.nhs.uk/live-well/, National Health Service advice on healthy living to prevent illness.

Walk 1,000 Miles *www.walk1000miles.co.uk*, advice and encouragement on improving fitness by walking.

USA

Medline Plus *https://medlineplus.gov/*, a federal medical information service.

Microsoft Health Information *https://www.msn.com/en-us/health*.

https://health.gov/, federal government information on healthy living.

Mayo Clinic *https://www.mayoclinic.org/*, comprehensive medical and health information.

Australia

Health Direct *https://www.healthdirect.gov.au/health-information-online*, government portal for trustworthy

online health information.
My Dr *https://www.mydr.com.au/*, commercial portal providing online health information
Life Program https://www.lifeprogram.org.au/living-well/healthy-living, free program in Victoria helping to reduce risk of type 2 diabetes and heart disease.

Canada

Health Canada/Healthy Living *https://www.canada.ca/en/health-canada.html*, government advice on healthy living.
Health Link BC *https://www.healthlinkbc.ca/*, British Columbia-based hub for health and medical information.
Healthy Families BC *https://www.healthyfamiliesbc.ca/*, British Columbia site giving general advice on healthy living.

Education and podcasts

International

Coursera *https://www.coursera.org/*, portal for education from universities, museums and companies around the world, some free.
Udemy *https://www.udemy.com/*, online video courses, some free.
Academic Earth *https://academicearth.org/*, free university-level courses.
TED-Ed *https://ed.ted.com/*, short educational talks.

UK

OpenLearn *https://www.open.edu/openlearn/*, the Open

University's free learning platform, with 1,000+ free courses.

Futurelearn *https://www.futurelearn.com/*, directory of online courses from UK and international universities.

University of Oxford Podcasts *https://podcasts.ox.ac.uk/*.

BBC Podcasts *https://www.bbc.co.uk/podcasts*.

BBC Radio 4 In Our Time *https://www.bbc.co.uk/programmes/b006qykl/episodes/player,* archive of discussions on a range of subjects, including recently John Wesley.

USA

Open Culture *https://www.openculture.com/*, portal for courses and lectures, many free.

LinkedIn Learning *www.linkedin.com/*, subscription-based online short courses.

Khan Academy *https://www.khanacademy.org/*, non-profit offering free courses, mostly at high school level.

EdX *https://www.edx.org/*, course from a range of colleges, some free.

iTunesU *https://itunesu.itunes.apple.com*, free online education delivered to Apple devices.

Carnegie Mellon Open Learning Initiative *https://oli.cmu.edu/*, free online education from Carnegie Mellon University.

Harvard Extension https://www.extension.harvard.edu, online courses offered by Harvard.

MIT OpenCourseWare https://ocw.mit.edu/, online courses offered by MIT.

Stanford Online *https://online.stanford.edu/*, online

courses offered by Stanford University.
UC Berkeley Class Central *https://extension.berkeley.edu*, online courses offered by Berkeley.
Open Yale Courses *https://oyc.yale.edu/*, online courses offered by Yale.
National Geographic Kids *https://kids.nationalgeographic.com/*, child-friendly education, organised by topic.

Personal finance software

I have been happy with Acemoney, a less well-known program available from www.mechcad.net, but alternatives include:

Quicken, an efficient and well-established program that operates across desktop, laptop and mobile phone.

Banktree, not especially user-friendly, but supports multiple currencies.

Money Dashboard, a free app for iOS or Android that links up to UK bank accounts.

YNAB, (You Need A Budget), which focuses on helping you keep your budgeting on track.

Moneydance, for Mac, iPhone and Windows, but not Android. Links to US but not UK banks.

Money (free) is another product that is more suitable for small business and can be used for 'proper' accounting, known as the 'accrual' basis as opposed to the 'cash' basis. If that is as clear as mud to you, don't let it worry you. It doesn't matter. Another small business option, also free, is Gnucash.

Further reading

The books listed here are either mentioned in the preceding chapters or relevant to the theme of the book. They are listed in reverse order of publication. Note the dates; some of the older books may be out of print and difficult to find, but I include them because they have stood the test of time.

Money before Marriage, John Ramsey (2020), a Christian look at financial preparation for marriage.

Renewing your Money Mind, Barbara Galloway (2020), a call to a biblical perspective on money.

Down Home Money, Myra Oliver (2020), an individual approach to financial freedom.

You of Little Faith, Ryan Thomas Holladay (2019), a call to radical and expectant giving.

Reset, David Sawyer (2018), ideas for achieving financial independence in mid-life.

Fast 800 and *The 8-week Blood Sugar Diet*, Dr Michael Moseley (2018, 2015) and *The 8-Week Blood Sugar Diet Recipe Book,* Dr Clare Bailey (2016), the science and health benefits of weight loss and reduced blood sugar, with advice on how to achieve both, and the companion recipe book.

John Wesley: A Brand from the Burning, Roy Hattersley (2017), biography of John Wesley.

The Life-Changing Magic of Tidying, Marie Kondo (2014), on systematic and radical decluttering.

God at Work, Ken Costa (2013), Christian faith in the workplace.

Millionaire Mind, Thomas Stanley (2002), exploring the

ideas, beliefs, and behaviours that have inspired millionaires.

Courage and Calling, Gordon Smith (1999), an examination of work, calling and vocation.

Hope has Wings, Stuart King (1993), the story of Mission Aviation Fellowship.

Your Money or Your Life, Vicki Robin and Joe Dominguez (1992), the trigger for the 'Financial Independence Retire Early' movement.

Living More Simply, edited by Ronald J Sider (1980), a collection of contributions on a simple lifestyle.

Rich Christians in an age of hunger, Ronald J. Sider (1977), a call to the church to recognise the need for global social justice.

Enough is Enough, John V Taylor (1975), a call to a battle against excess.

Hidden Art, Edith Schaeffer (1972), the story of a beautiful home created on a minimal budget.

The Cost of Discipleship, Dietrich Bonhoeffer (1959 translation of 1933 *Nachfolge*), an uncompromising look at the Christian life.

Budget Categories

You can use this list of budget categories in several ways. if you are comfortable working in a spreadsheet, you can simply paste the whole list into a column and then make any adjustments you wish, to suit your personal circumstances. Alternatively, you can use the list as an aide memoire as you set up your personal finance program.

Main headings are followed by sub-headings. I can't claim that the list is comprehensive. You will probably think of things to add, or define categories differently. But Iit's a good starting point.

Income

Salary
Bonuses
Consultancy Income
Expenses and Allowances Received
Sales Income
Gifts Received
Rent Received
Investment: Dividends; Interest
Miscellaneous Income

Spending

Utilities: Electricity; Water and Sewerage; Gas; Telephone; Recycling/Waste
Internet: Mobile Phone/Cell phone; Broadband; Cable TV; Satellite TV
Food and Drink: :Groceries; Eating out; Restaurants;

Coffee

Home: Rent/Mortgage Payments; Council Tax/Property Taxes; Home improvement and Maintenance; Home Security Gardening Expenses

Household: Household Supplies; Tools; Kitchen Equipment; Appliance Purchase/Replacement; Cleaning Supplies

Finance and Legal: Student Loan Payments; Personal Loan Payments; Credit Card Payments; Bank Charges/Fees; Interest;

Financial advisor; Legal Advice; Tax Advisor

Insurance: Life Insurance; Buildings and Contents Insurance; Personal Effects and Property Insurance; Disability Insurance

Travel: Car Loan/Lease Payments; Car Insurance; Fuel; Car Maintenance; Parking Fees; Toll Fees; Vehicle Registration Fees; Roadside Assistance; Public Transport Fares; Taxi

Health: Medical Insurance; Dental Insurance; Prescription Charges; Medication and Vitamins; Gym Membership; Physiotherapy; Counselling

Pets: Pet Food; Pet insurance; Veterinary Care; Pet Medication

Personal: Hairdresser/Barber; Toiletries; Cosmetics

Clothing: Clothes; Shoes; Laundry/Dry Cleaning

Gifts and charitable giving: Charities (specify); Church; Personal/Family Gifts (Birthdays, Anniversaries, Weddings, Special Occasions)

Professional: Work Clothes; Professional Development/Training; Professional/Union Fees;

Computer Equipment

Education: Tuition Fees; School Fees; School Supplies; School Uniform; Field Trips

Family: Childcare; Babysitting

Recreation and Entertainment: Sports; Vacation/Holiday Travel, Accommodation and Food; Events; Cinema; Theatre; Hobbies and Crafts; Books; Newspapers and Magazines

Savings [for]: Emergency Fund; Retirement; Housing; Education; Car Replacement; Medical Costs; Vacation

John Wesley's 'The Use of Money'

John Wesley's Sermon

SERMON XLIV
THE USE OF MONEY

I say unto you, Make to yourselves friends of the mammon of unrighteousness; that, when ye fail, they may receive you into everlasting habitations.—LUKE xvi. 9.

OUR Lord, having finished the beautiful parable of the Prodigal Son, which He had particularly addressed to those who murmured at His receiving publicans and sinners, adds another relation of a different kind, addressed rather to the children of God. 'He said unto His disciples'—not so much to the Scribes and Pharisees, to whom He had been speaking before—'There was a certain rich man, who had a steward, and he was accused to him of wasting his goods. And calling him, he said, Give an account of thy stewardship for thou canst be no longer steward' (verses 1, 2). After reciting the method which the bad steward used to provide against the day of necessity, our Saviour adds, 'His lord commended the unjust steward'; namely, in this respect, that he used timely precaution; and subjoins this weighty reflection, 'The children of this world are wiser in their generation than the children of light' (verse 8): those who seek no other portion than this world 'are wiser' (not absolutely; for they are, one and all, the veriest fools, the most egregious madmen under heaven; but, 'in their generation,' in their own way; they are more consistent with themselves; they are truer to their acknowledged principles; they more steadily pursue their end) 'than the children of light,'—than they who see 'the light of the glory of God in the face of Jesus Christ.' Then follow the words above recited: 'And I'—the only-begotten Son of

John Wesley's Sermon 'The Use of Money', 1787

John Wesley is said to have preached more than 40,000 sermons, living frugally and travelling on horseback from place to place. His sermons were then and still are popular. It is not clear when Wesley first preached his sermon on 'The Use of Money'.

He preached on the sermon's text, Luke 16:9, on 17th February 1744 in London, and subsequently in Newcastle-upon-Tyne, Bristol, Bradford-on-Avon, Dublin, Cork and many other places - in all more than two dozen times - but the sermon may not have been exactly the one published. He first published 'The Use of Money' in 1760. Its first page is reproduced here from the fourth edition of his Sermons on Several Occasions, printed in 1787.

John Wesley's 'The Use of Money' in Modern English[25]

I tell you, use worldly wealth to gain friends for yourself, so that when it is gone, you will be welcomed into eternal dwellings." Luke 16:9

The right use of money is of the utmost importance to the Christian, yet it is a subject given too little attention. Wealth has often been regarded by poets and philosophers as a source of evil and yet the fault lies, not with money, but with those who use it. Indeed, money should be regarded as a gift of God for the benefits that it brings in ordering the affairs of civilization and the opportunities it offers for doing good. In the hands of God's children, money is food for the hungry, clothing for

---

[25] An abridgement in modern English by Richard Hall, (www.shropshireandmarches.org.uk/whos-who/richard-hall.html).

the naked and shelter for the stranger. With money we can care for the widow and the fatherless, defend the oppressed, meet the need of those who are sick or in pain.

It is therefore most urgent that God's people know how to make use of their money for his glory. All the necessary instructions can be condensed into 3 simple rules:

GAIN ALL YOU CAN
SAVE ALL YOU CAN
GIVE ALL YOU CAN

Gain all you can

With this first rule, we sound like children of the world, and it is our bounden duty to do this. There are, however, limits to this rule. We should not gain money at the expense of life or health. No sum of money, however large, should induce us to accept employment which would injure our bodies. Neither should we begin (or continue in) any business which deprives us of the food and sleep that we need. We may draw a distinction between businesses which are absolutely unhealthy, such as those that deal directly with dangerous materials, and those employments which would be harmful to those of a weak constitution. If our reason or experience shows that a job is unhealthy for us, then we should leave it as soon as possible even if this means that our income is reduced.

The rule is further limited by the necessity not to undertake any employment which might injure our minds. This includes the pursuit of any trade which is against the law of God or the law of the land. It is just as wrong to defraud the king of taxes as it is to steal from our fellow citizens. There are businesses which might be innocent in themselves but which, at least in England at this time require cheating, lying or other customs which are contrary to good conscience, to provide an adequate income. These, too, we should avoid. There are other trades which many may pursue with complete innocence but which you may not because of some peculiarity of your nature. For example, I am convinced that I could not study mathematics without losing my faith, yet many others pursue a lifetime study in that field without harm. Everyone must judge for themselves and refrain from whatever may harm their mind and soul.

What is true of ourselves is equally true of our neighbour. We should not "gain all we can" by causing injury to another, whether to his trade, his body or his soul. We should not sell our goods below their market price nor should we entice away, or receive, the workers' that a brother has need of. It is quite wrong to make a living from selling those things which would harm a neighbour's health and physicians should not deliberately prolong a patient's illness in order to improve his own income.

With these restrictions, it is every Christian's duty to observe this first rule:

'Gain all you can'.

Gain all you can by honest work with all diligence. Lose no time in silly diversions and do not put off until tomorrow what may be done today. Do nothing by halves; use all the common sense that God has given you and study continually that you may improve on those who have gone before you. Make the best of all that is in your hands.

Save all you can

This is the second rule. Money is a precious gift. It should not be wasted on trivialities. Do not spend money on luxury foods, but be content with simple things that your body needs. Ornaments too, whether of the body, house or garden are a waste and should be avoided. Do not spend in order to gratify your vanity or to gain the admiration of others. The more you feed your pride in this way, the more it will grow within you.

And why should you spoil your children in this way? Fine clothes and luxury are a snare to them as they are to you. Why would you want to provide them with more pride and vanity? They have enough already! If you have good reason to believe that they would waste your wealth then do not leave it to them. Do not tempt them in this way. I am amazed at those parents who think that they can never leave their children enough. Have they no fear of hell? If there is only one child in the family who knows the value of money and there is a fortune to be inherited, then it is that one who should receive the bulk of it. If no child can be trusted in this way then it is the Christian's duty to leave them only what will keep them from being in need. The rest should be distributed in order to bring glory to God.

Give all you can

Observing the first two rules is far from enough. Storing away money without using it is to throw it away. You might just as well cast your money into the sea as keep it in the bank. Having gained and saved all you can, then give all you can.

Why is this? You do not own the wealth that you have. It has been entrusted to you for a short while by the God who brought you into being. All belongs to him. Your wealth is to be used for him as a holy sacrifice, made acceptable through Jesus Christ.

If you wish to be a good steward of that which God has given to you on loan the rules are simple enough. First provide sufficient food and clothing for yourself and your household. If there is a surplus after this is done, then use what remains for the good of your Christian brothers and sisters. If there is still a surplus, then do good to all people, as you have the opportunity. If at any time you have a doubt about any particular expenditure, ask yourself honestly:

> Will I be acting, not as an owner, but as a steward of the Lord's goods?

> Am I acting in obedience to the word of God?

> Is this expense a sacrifice to God through Jesus Christ?

> Do I believe that this expense will bring reward at the day of resurrection?

If you are still in doubt, put these questions as statements to God in prayer: "Lord, you see that I am going to spend this money on ... and you know that I am acting as your trusted steward according to your design." If you can make this prayer with a good conscience then you will know that your expense is right and good.

These, then, are the simple rules for the Christian use

of money. Gain all you can, without bringing harm to yourself or neighbour. Save all you can by avoiding waste and unnecessary luxuries. Finally, give all you can. Do not limit yourself to a proportion. Do not give God a tenth or even half what he already owns, but give all that is his by using your wealth to preserve yourself and family, the Church of God and the rest of humanity. In this way you will be able to give a good account of your stewardship when the Lord comes with all his saints.

I plead with you in the name of the Lord Jesus, no more delay! Whatever task is before you, do it with all your strength. No more waste or luxury or envy. Use whatever God has loaned to you to do good to your fellow Christians and to all people. Give all that you have, as well as all that you are, to him who did not even withhold his own Son for your sake.

ABOUT THE AUTHOR

Dr Peter Dixon is a researcher, lecturer and nonfiction author. He served for over 30 years as a Royal Air Force pilot and spent the next decade leading the charity Concordis International in its conflict resolution work in Sudan and other divided societies. He completed a PhD at the University of Cambridge in 2015 on intervention in civil wars.

He and his wife Ingrid, also an author, work from their home in Gloucestershire, England, when their five grandchildren allow them to do so.

www.ingramcontent.com/pod-product-compliance
Lightning Source LLC
Chambersburg PA
CBHW071517080526
44588CB00011B/1464